BEER

The Practical Guide to Exploring Craft Beer

and Improving Physical and Mental Fitness

By Matthew John Benecke

Title: Beer & Fitness: The Practical Guide to Exploring Craft Beer and Improving Physical and Mental Fitness

Author: Matthew John Benecke

Email: matthewjohnbenecke@gmail.com

Website: http://www.matthewjohnbenecke.com

Copyright © 2017 by Matthew John Benecke

ISBN-10: 1542818389
ISBN-13: 978-1542818384

ACKNOWLEDGEMENTS

Without the physical therapy of Susan Medford I wouldn't be where I am today. She literally helped me to get back onto my feet after a catastrophic ankle injury and set me on the path that ultimately led not just to my recovery but to my self-improvement as well. Her guidance, friendship, and professional care have proven invaluable over the past few years and I humbly thank her and the rest of the staff at Professional Physical Therapy for all that they have done for me.

I'd like to thank my good buddy Dave Schwartz for his continued friendship and interest in craft beer. His unbridled enthusiasm and genuine interest in learning more about craft beer inspired me to deepen my own understanding and has transformed what was at times a latent hobby into a full blown passion. His generosity is unmatched and I consider myself fortunate to have met him and to consider him a part of our family as well.

Stanley Lee is a perpetual source of inspiration for me and embodies all of the characteristics and qualities that I champion in the fitness section of this book. He is a man whose intellect and physical prowess are surpassed only by his compassion and inimitable magnanimity. Stan is living proof that with hard work and determination one can bring about and maintain meaningful changes to one's lifestyle and perspective.

Thanks to Nightcharges, Seabranddesign, and Shineonoat on www.vecteezy.com for the Free Beer Vector image and Free Dumbbell Vector images

DEDICATION

I dedicate this book to my wonderful wife Heather because of her longstanding interest in craft beer and her unwavering support of me. Most of my 3,500+ different craft beers have been shared with her including the "Beers of the World" pack that started us on this incredible journey. Her support of me in all things that I do provides the foundation upon which I have built my life and has given me the confidence in myself that I can achieve the things that I dream of doing. Her belief in me played an enormous role in my physical transformation and enabled me not just to get back to the fitness levels of my adolescence but to *surpass* them.

Heathe—you make this life worth living and I wouldn't be who I am or where I am today without you. I love you and thank you for all that you do for me and our family!

DISCLAIMER

I do not have a professional background in nutrition and thus make no claims as to the safety and efficacy of the health advice provided herein. It is highly advisable that you consult a medical professional before making any significant changes in diet and exercise including and especially any such changes inspired by the information in Beer & Fitness: The Practical Guide to Exploring Craft Beer and Improving Physical and Mental Fitness. The information is meant merely to serve as an example of one person's successful route to healthier living and cannot and should not substitute the care and guidance of licensed, experienced medical professionals.

TABLE OF CONTENTS

BEER & FITNESS

We are living in the Golden Age of beer in the United States. Never before have we enjoyed more variety and quality in our beer options. Innovation is at an all-time high and thus the product that reaches our palates has evolved well beyond the insipid, uninspired fizzy yellow brew of yore. Sure there is room at the table for "Big Beer" and their macrobrews but the panoply of passion-infused, imaginative beers is growing exponentially.

Unfortunately, as our list of beer options grows so too do our waistlines. According to the Center for Disease Control and Prevention, more than one-third (36.5% or 116.4 million) of Americans are obese resulting in an estimated annual medical cost of $147 billion.[1] By comparison, the overall beer market in the United States in 2015 generated $105.9 billion in revenue.[2] This means that more tax dollars were spent treating obesity related medical expenses than hard earned income was spent on beer!

Beer drinking is often unfairly associated with being overweight with the stereotypical "beer gut" being the iconic image that many people have of beer drinkers. Many factors contribute to obesity and though the consumption of beer might be counted among them it is hardly the chief offender. In fact, I would argue that obesity rates have as much to do with *how* we consume as with what we put into our bodies.

Whether it's beer or junk food—soda or sweets, the overconsumption of empty calories without proper exercise and supplemental nutrition will undoubtedly lead to weight gain. I experienced this first-hand by putting on nearly seventy pounds between the time I started college and the time I finally admitted to myself that my lifestyle was unhealthy. I ate poorly and drank a lot, especially after finding and falling in love with craft beer; it was just easier to be that way than it was to change.

Many people are creatures of habit who find comfort in convenience; as such we have become victims of access and excess. We binge on things that bring us pleasure whether it is craft beer and fast food or television shows and social media. We also have an incredibly difficult time enacting healthy changes in our lives.

Losing weight and living a healthier lifestyle is at best an uphill battle for many Americans. We are easily discouraged and envious of those who seem to have it all figured out while many of us lack the willpower and conviction to make seemingly simple adjustments to our habits. We are encouraged to be healthier and fitter but are given neither the tools necessary nor the proper framework with which to do so.

Though I cannot claim to have all of the answers or provide some magic elixir for weight-loss and self-improvement I *can* provide the perspective of someone who struggled with these issues and who found the way finally to make a change. In the process, I made very few daunting, drastic changes to my lifestyle and instead found a way of fitting the things that I loved the most into a healthier way of eating, thinking, and being. My relationship with craft beer is a huge part of how I was able to make those changes; it was the one thing above everything else that I refused to give up.

Between 2007 and the present, I have tried more than 3,500 different beers. More than half of those were consumed between 2007 and February 2013. At that time I weighed 230 pounds and felt as awful as I looked. Then, I took the first steps towards finally slimming down and, more importantly, being healthier. Since then, I have added more than **1,800** new beers to my list while simultaneously shedding almost *fifty* pounds. More importantly, I have kept that weight off while leading a very active lifestyle both in terms of physical exercise and responsible craft beer consumption.

In this book I will explore my journey with you and explain how I was able to maintain an ardent craft beer passion and still live a healthy lifestyle without feeling deprived or exerting excessive effort. The first half will guide you through exploring craft beer as a hobby while the latter will delve into fitness and how to create harmony between the two. After all, there's no reason why we shouldn't be able to enjoy craft beer *and* stay fit as well!

A BRIEF INTRODUCTION TO CRAFT BEER

Craft beer is one of the fastest growing industries in the United States contributing more than $55.7 billion dollars to the national economy and creating more than 424,000 jobs in 2014 alone.[3] In 2012 there were just under 2,500 breweries in the United States; by 2015 that number skyrocketed to nearly *4,300*—an increase of more than **72%**.[4] This, during a time when the overall economy is still weak and many small businesses are shuttering their doors! According to the Small Business Association, between 2009 and 2013 there were 2,015,802 startups (firms less than one year old) and 2,108,365 closures resulting in a net loss of nearly 100,000 businesses or a net *decrease* of nearly 5%.[5] By comparison, the Brewers Association states that between 2010 and 2015 2,924 brewpubs and microbreweries opened to only 363 closures—a net *increase* of nearly **90%**.[6] That means that for every one craft brewpub or microbrewery that closed there were nine more that opened!

Inc. magazine, which ranks annually the 5,000 fastest-growing private companies in the United States, featured nearly a dozen breweries on its 2015 list.[7] Seven of these posted growth of more than 120% with Figueroa Mountain Brewing Co. leading the pack with a staggering increase of 893% and ranking them number 519 out of 5,000. Stone Brewing Co., one of the most well-known breweries in the United States, made the top 3,000 with growth of 121% and total revenue of $185.7 million placing them first in earnings among the breweries listed. Not bad for an industry that is still only just now growing in mainstream popularity!

WHAT IS BEER?

Over the past few decades, craft beer has grown from a collection of niche breweries and homebrewers into a thriving community of beer lovers. Still, many people are unfamiliar with the term craft beer and its meaning. In order to define *craft* beer we must first delve into what makes beer *beer* in the first place. (Note: There are many, *many* tomes available that cover the history of beer in far greater detail than I will here. The purpose of this book is to provide an entry point for folks who are curious about craft beer or who are just getting into it as a hobby. For anyone who is interested in learning more about the minutiae of beer please explore the Further Reading section at the back of the book.)

Beer is at once endlessly complex and remarkably simple. It takes only four ingredients to make it but the variety and variation within those elements allows for an incredibly diverse spectrum of styles. Factor in the seemingly endless array of adjunct ingredients that can be added and you begin to get a sense of the vast scope of offerings available in the modern market.

At its core, beer is comprised of water, malted cereal grain (barley most often), hops, and yeast. Water represents the single largest component of beer while the malts, hops, and yeast provide for the greatest amount of control over variety and differentiation. The malts in particular provide the color and body of the beer while the hops determine the bitterness level, act as a preservative, and add additional flavoring. The yeast generates the alcohol but it can also affect the flavor particularly between lagers and ales and between Belgian and other styles of beer.

As you might expect, different water sources, types of grains and hops, and strains of yeast will produce different characteristics in the beer that is brewed. Some water types are better suited for certain styles such as the hard water in Dublin for brewing stout and the soft water of the Czech Republic for making pilsners.[8] With that said, water is the most difficult component to manipulate as brewers are often limited geographically and geologically by their local water sources. This often imbues their beers with a distinct regional quality that serves to differentiate them even within their established styles.

The type of malted grain used has an enormous impact on the color, flavor, and mouthfeel (texture) of the beer. Malting refers to the process of drying grains to generate sugar-producing enzymes.[9] These enzymes break down the starch in the grain into sugars while others break down the grain's protein into usable forms for the yeast. Both of these elements are necessary for the creation of alcohol and carbonization in the beer.

A single beer recipe can call for multiple types of starch sources in differing amounts; this collection is referred to as the grain bill and serves to determine how light or dark a beer will be in terms of color and how sweet or roasted it will be in terms of flavor.[10] Roasting temperatures and durations can elicit different colors and characteristics from the same grain though darker source malts will always produce darker beers. Generally, the longer the malt is roasted and the higher the temperature, the darker and bolder the resulting beer will be. Proper kilning is crucial to creating the sweeter caramel and toffee notes of certain beer styles: roasted for too long or at too high a temperature and the resulting malt can become bitter and burned.

Hops provide the balancing bitterness to the malt's sweetness. They affect the smell of the beer (referred to as the nose or bouquet) and contribute an array of aromas ranging from tropical and citrusy to grassy and floral. Bitterness is determined by the acid components of the hops and when the hops are added during the brewing process. Certain hop strains are ideal for providing a bitter backbone to the beer while others are better utilized for improving the beer's bouquet. Employing hop varietals in combination can also yield different results through their interplay.

Yeast has the single most important job in the beer making process: producing alcohol and carbon dioxide. It works in conjunction with the malts, metabolizing the sugars extracted from the grains thereby fermenting the beer. Typically brewing yeasts are used when making beer as these strains are vitamin-rich and produce fewer undesirable flavors and characteristics than other strains.[11]

The strain of yeast used also determines the primary categorization of the beer. Lagers are brewed with bottom-fermenting (or bottom-cropping) yeast, which means that the yeast settles at the bottom of the vessel during fermentation.[12] Lager beer is also cool fermented at around 50 °F—about 14 degrees cooler than ales and a temperature at which most top-fermenting yeasts become dormant. The use of lager yeast such as *Saccharomyces pastorianus* and colder temperatures will result in a beer that is both cleaner-looking and crisper-tasting.

Ales by contrast are brewed using top-fermenting (or top cropping) yeast such as *Saccharomyces cerevisiae* that clump and rise to the surface during fermentation. Ale yeast ferments more rapidly than its lager counterpart and at higher temperatures through the process of warm fermentation.[13] The resulting beer contains so-called fruity esters that affect both the aroma and the taste. It is also more complex in flavor and fuller-bodied than a beer fermented with lager yeast.[14] *Saccharomyces cerevisiae* was made the official state microbe of Oregon in 2013 to honor its importance in the brewing process and to recognize the impact that craft beer has had on the state's economy and identity.[15]

Lambics and sour ales represent beers brewed with a third strain of yeast and fermentation method. These styles are fermented spontaneously meaning that the wort (the liquid that holds the sugars to be converted into alcohol by the yeast) is exposed to the air and allowed to be infiltrated by yeast and bacteria from the surrounding environment. *Brettanomyces* is the strain of yeast most often used in spontaneous fermentation and is occasionally coupled with bacteria such as *Lactobacillus* or *Pediococcus* to produce tart, sour qualities in the beer.[16] It is also well-known for producing barnyard flavors and aromas—elements that necessitate an acquired taste!

THE BREWING PROCESS:

MASHING & LAUTERING

Anyone who has ever taken a brewery tour has likely heard about the brewing process. For those of you who are new to the game though I believe that it is an important inclusion in this book to help you to understand beer—both micro- and macrobrewed—better. It is a fairly simple and straightforward process but one in which a keen eye for detail can yield incredible results.

Every batch of beer regardless of style begins with water. For larger breweries this water is heated in a vessel called a mash tun. The milled and malted grains are added to the hot water to steep for a period of time (usually no longer than two hours) while keeping the temperature below 170 °F; this process is called mashing and the resulting combination of water and grains, the mash. By steeping the grains in water at the target temperature the brewer is able to convert the starches into sugar, which will serve as food for the yeast later in the process; too high or low a temperature inhibits this conversion and can prevent the yeast from obtaining enough material to use in its alcohol production.

After an hour or two, the water and extracted sugars have combined to create a liquid known as wort. This is essentially the base of the beer and bears a characteristically sweet, pleasant aroma that is instantly recognizable at breweries (or a homebrewer's kitchen!) In order to transform the wort into beer however it must be separated from the mash in a process called lautering.

Lautering consists of three steps: mashout, recirculation, and sparging.[17] During the mashout, the mash *is* raised to 170 °F in order to halt the starch conversion into sugars. The additional heat also serves to liquefy the wort further making it easier to separate it from the solids. At this point, the mash is either transferred to a separate lauter tun for the remaining steps or, if a combination mash-lauter tun was used, it stays in place. Either way, the lauter tun or combination mash-lauter tun has a false or slotted bottom that allows the liquid wort to be extracted while leaving the solid grains behind.

During lautering, a portion of the wort will be drained from the bottom and poured back on top of the grain bed in a process called recirculation. This serves to filter some of the bits of grain and debris that must be removed prior to the boiling stage thereby clarifying the liquid wort. Though lauter tuns have slotted or false bottoms, it is actually the mash itself that filters out the wort by collecting the bits of protein and debris much like a sand filter.[18]

Sparging, the final step in the lautering process, begins after the bulk of the wort has been drained. The remaining collection of grains is rinsed with hot water to extract as much of the remaining sugars as possible while once again keeping a keen eye on the temperature. If the sparging water is too hot (higher than 170 °F) then unwanted materials called tannins might be released into the wort thereby making the beer bitter and astringent. This is a critical step in the lautering process though and ultimately worth the risk as it helps to maximize the yield; after all, more wort means more beer!

THE BOIL

Now fully separated from the grains, the liquid wort is pumped to a brew kettle to be boiled. Most modern breweries use stainless steel brew kettles though copper was favored historically. Copper is a better conductor of heat and does not allow steam bubbles to adhere to its surface but stainless steel is more affordable and stands up better to the brewing process and the often caustic cleaning agents used to maintain brewery equipment.[19] The main drawback with steel though is the danger of overheating during boiling, which can caramelize or burn the sugars in the wort thus negatively affecting the flavor of the finished beer.[20]

At this stage, the wort is brought to a boil and kept at that temperature for anywhere from 45 to 90 minutes or longer depending upon the type of beer being brewed.[21] A rolling or continuous boil that maintains steady intensity is used to sterilize the wort as well as to allow for the various chemical processes that must occur during this phase. Sterilization removes any microbes or unwanted bacteria that could potentially ruin the final beer's flavor. This is critical because even trace amounts of these uninvited guests can cause a beer to suffer from off-flavors or to taste infected (sourness in a beer that's not meant to be sour).

Boiling serves a second, equally important function: it is the point at which hops are introduced. Hops are added at varying points in the boil to produce different effects in the beer: bitterness is contributed earlier in the boil while aroma and hop flavor come from later additions. The effects themselves are also determined by the two types of acids found in hops—alpha and beta—as well as the essential oils.[22] Alpha acids determine a beer's bitterness while the beta acids and essential oils impart hop aroma and hop taste.[23] Consequently, certain hop cultivars are employed at specific points in the boil to elicit the desired result.

Bittering hops are those that are particularly high in alpha acids. The resin from these acids is what provides the bitterness but it must first be isomerized by boiling the liquid wort.[24] Isomerization (the process that transforms one molecule into another with the exact same atoms but in a different arrangement) is directly affected by the length of the boil: the more time the hops spend being boiled, the greater the isomerization percentage and thus the greater the bitterness. A longer boil also allows for the evaporation of the hops' essential oils (the elements that provide both the hop aroma and flavor), which means that hops high in alpha acids added at the beginning of the boil will ultimately provide bitterness and little else.

Aroma hops by contrast are lower in alpha acids, generally higher in beta acids, and feature more prominent essential oils. Though beta acids contribute to the beer's bouquet it is ultimately the essential oils that impart the most flavor and aroma. These oils are comprised of delicate compounds that do not stand up well to the rigor of a rolling boil. As a result, aroma hops are added later in the process (typically during the final thirty minutes) to preserve their aromatic and flavoring qualities.

Aroma hops can be further broken down into flavoring and finishing hops. Flavoring hops are usually added during the final thirty minutes of the boil while the finishing hops come during the final ten to fifteen minutes. The latter provide an intense burst of hop aroma due to the lack of evaporation of the essential oils while the former donate the pleasant herbal flavor characteristic of hops. A knowledgeable brewer can create a complex beer with the right combination of hops added at the appropriate times.

The inclusion and subsequent breakdown of hops (and any other flavoring ingredients) during the boil results in a significant amount of solid particles in the wort. This collection of debris is called trub and must be separated from the liquid before fermentation begins.[25] A whirlpool effect is generated to drive the trub towards the bottom-center of the tank through centripetal force; this allows for easy removal of the solid sediment before the liquid is transferred into the fermenter.

COOLING & FERMENTING

Once the wort has been separated from the trub, it must be cooled preferably at a rapid pace. Yeast is sensitive to heat and cold and will not perform its function properly (or at all) at too high a temperature therefore it is critical to cool the wort before pitching the yeast. Wort that is left too warm or exposed to open air at too high a temperature can also become infected with bacteria; this is more of an issue for home brewers than commercial ones since these larger breweries make use of equipment that transfers the wort without exposing it to the surrounding environment.

Most modern breweries cool their wort by using a plate heat exchanger, which can lower the temperature of the liquid rapidly and significantly.[26] In a plate heat exchanger, the wort is pumped into one side while a cooling liquid (usually water) is pumped into another. The two liquids are separated by the plates in their own passageways and never come into direct contact with one another. Instead, as they wind their way through the labyrinth of plates, their respective temperatures are altered by one another: the hot wort transfers its heat into the water through the plates and the chilled water cools down the wort by absorbing its heat. Many breweries will preserve the hot water for later use thereby increasing efficiency and reducing waste.[27]

The now-chilled wort is aerated and pumped into a fermenter to begin fermentation. Introducing oxygen into the wort is an important step because it helps to foster growth and reproduction of the yeast as it feeds on the sugars.[28] The yeast is then added (pitched, in beer-speak) to the wort inside of the fermentation vessel. For most commercial breweries, this is typically a large, closed, conical, stainless-steel container called a CCV (cylindroconical vessel). The shape of this vessel (conical at the bottom, cylindrical at the top), allows the yeast and other sediment to fall to the apex (or bottom) and then to be flushed out when fermentation is complete.

During fermentation, the yeast feeds upon the sugars in the wort and converts them into both alcohol and carbon dioxide. This is an active process that can generate a good deal of gas and thus pressure inside of the fermenter. Most CCVs use a blow-off tube that is placed into a bucket of water to allow the carbon dioxide to bubble out. [29] Aside from reducing pressure inside of the fermenter this also serves as an indicator that active fermentation is still occurring:

bubbling water means that the yeast are still consuming the sugars and creating alcohol.[30]

Primary fermentation is considered to be complete when most of the fermentable sugars have been consumed—evidenced by a lack of vigorous bubbling in the water bucket. At this point, much of the yeast has likely settled and can be drawn out. Not all of the cells have become dormant however nor has all of the edible material been consumed; it is at this point that secondary fermentation can begin.

Secondary fermentation can occur either in the same fermenter or in a separate conditioning vessel. Additional sugars can be added to feed the remaining yeast cells or the beer can be Kräusened by adding a small amount of still-fermenting wort to the completed beer.[31] This spurs the yeast cells to generate more alcohol, to carbonate the beer (by this time trapping the gas inside of the conditioning vessel), and to rid the beer of fermenting by-products thereby cleaning it.[32] More hops can be added at this point to contribute aroma to the final beer through a process called dry hopping.

Dry hopping is an important step in producing a beer with potent hop aromas. Some breweries will dry hop in a secondary fermentation vessel while others opt to do so in the primary fermenter once fermentation has completed. It can be a process as simple as opening the top of the fermenter and dumping the hops in (which, consequently, exposes the beer however briefly to the environment and unwanted oxygen) or it can be a more complicated, sophisticated affair. Carton Brewing in Atlantic Highlands, New Jersey, for example, makes use of a device called the BrauKon HopGun that recirculates the finished beer through hop pellets. This creates the effect of a weeklong dry hopping session in a matter of hours and can drastically reduce the amount of material that needs to be filtered out of the beer before packaging.

CONDITIONING & CARBONATION

With fermentation complete, the beer is now ready to be conditioned. This process can last for as little as a few days or as long as a year or more depending upon the brewer's intention. Conditioning serves a variety of purposes: it allows the beer to mature and develop, to clarify and improve its aesthetics, and to carbonate, among others.[33] Most breweries will filter their beer prior to conditioning to achieve greater clarity but some opt to provide their beers in an unfiltered more natural state.

Once fully-fermented and filtered, the now-clarified beer (called bright beer because of its clearer, less cloudy appearance) is pumped into a bright (or "brite") beer tank. The beer then conditions in the brite tank where it clears up further, gains flavor complexity, and becomes carbonated. There are numerous methods used to carbonate beer but many breweries will opt for direct injection of carbon dioxide into the brite tank because of the time it saves (carbonation that would take two weeks to complete can now be finished in only a day).

Another popular approach to carbonating beer is the use of bottle conditioning. The flat, finished beer is placed into bottles that have small amounts of priming sugar added and, in some cases, additional yeast pitched. This kick-starts the yeast back into action causing it to produce more alcohol and carbon dioxide. With the beer bottled and capped however the gas has nowhere to go and is in turn forced to dissolve into the liquid thereby carbonating it. Because bottle conditioned beers have active yeast and sugars inside of them they benefit from long-term aging and will develop different characteristics over time as compared with traditionally filtered and carbonated ones.[34]

BOTTLING & BARREL AGING

Most non-bottle conditioned beer is ready at this point to be bottled, canned, or kegged and shipped out for consumption. Some very lucky beer though will spend some additional time aging in wooden barrels. Oftentimes these barrels (usually oak) previously held some sort of wine or spirit—be it whiskey, rum, brandy, or tequila. Remnants of these liquids remain trapped inside of the wood's pores and will impart their essence to the beer it comes in contact with.

Wood expands and contracts as a result of temperature fluctuations pulling liquid into the empty spaces within the staves and imbuing it with its scents and flavors. It then releases it to blend with the rest of the spirit or beer before absorbing it once again. This process mellows out the alcoholic punch of the liquid and creates delectable complexity that simply cannot be achieved through any other method.

Oak is most commonly used for aging spirits and subsequently beer. The type of oak and the degree of toasting of the wood ultimately determines what characteristics wind up in the aged beer. American and French oak are the two most popular types used and offer notes of coconut and butterscotch along with vanilla and caramel overtones depending upon the level of toasting.[35] The wood itself can also be tasted in the beer—a quality that can serve either to enhance the overall flavor or to dominate and destroy the nuances. Time spent in the barrel and environmental conditions such as temperature and humidity have an enormous impact on what types of flavors and aromas get contributed to the final beer.

Of course, repeat usage of a barrel ultimately diminishes its ability to impart these desirable qualities. As a result, barrels might be used only once or at most several times before being repurposed or discarded. Barrel-aged beers, consequently, are often highly sought after and sold at a premium because of their scarcity and the brewery's production limitations. I am a huge fan of barrel aged beers because of the additional layers of flavor and complexity they have as compared with their traditionally conditioned brethren.

THE DIFFERENCE BETWEEN MACROBREWED AND

MICROBREWED:

BIG BEER VERSUS CRAFT BEER

We've discussed what makes beer beer...but what exactly is *craft* beer? According to the Brewers Association—a respected resource in the world of craft beer—it is made by small, independent, innovative breweries that meet certain production and ownership criteria. Statistically speaking, this constitutes any brewery making less than 6 million barrels of beer and one that is less than 25% owned or controlled by an alcoholic beverage industry member that is not itself a craft brewer.[36]

Personally, I find the less tangible aspects to be more important to the definition, namely innovation. To me, a craft brewer is a small, independently owned brewery that offers its own unique spin on traditional beer styles and/or that seeks to innovate by developing new styles, techniques, or ingredient combinations. A craft brewer pays the utmost attention not just to the quality of the end product but also to that of the component ingredients; a willingness to experiment and a desire to broaden one's brewing horizons demonstrate the spirit of what makes craft beer great. For craft brewers, beer is as much their creative outlet as it is a source of income.

Craft beer is the umbrella term that covers several brewing subsets, chiefly microbreweries, nanobreweries, and brewpubs. The Brewers Association defines a microbrewery as producing less than 15,000 barrels of beer and selling more than three-quarters of that beer off-site.[37] One barrel of beer is the equivalent of 31 gallons or just under 250 standard pints; fifteen thousand barrels amounts to little in the overall beer market.[38]

There is no clear line of delineation for when a microbrewery can be considered a nanobrewery but general consensus is that a nanobrewery produces only a *few* barrels of beer. Its degree of distribution is also extremely limited—usually to a very small geographic area local to the brewery. Typically, nanobrewery setups are more comparable to home brewing than the state-of-the-art technology and equipment employed by larger craft brewers.

A brewpub, by comparison, can produce larger quantities of beer but it must sell the majority of its beer on premises. I have always thought of a brewpub as a location that brews its own beer, sells it chiefly for consumption on-site, and serves its own food.

Interestingly enough, there is little to no mention of food as a requirement for the definition though brewpubs are often referred to as restaurants or pubs that brew their own beer.

Typically, brewpubs *do* serve food and because of their status as a combination brewery-restaurant, brewing space is often supremely limited. The result then is that very little beer if any is bottled or canned due to the space required for the requisite equipment. Instead, beer that is served to-go is often dispensed directly into thick glass vessels called growlers; individual state laws (which vary greatly from state to state) ultimately determine how much beer can be sold to go at brewpubs and in what manner it may be dispensed.

Early on, the microbrewery designation was critical to differentiating smaller-scale brewers from their giant macro-counterparts but it has since become a relic of a bygone era. Many of the most iconic microbreweries of yore have grown exponentially since their births and can no longer be labeled as such; instead, they are considered craft brewers. This term too may undergo a degree of change in the future as production continues to expand due to the demand for and popularity of the beers they make. In the past decade or so alone the amount of qualifying beer has risen from one million barrels to six million![39]

Macrobreweries on the other hand account for the majority of the beer sold in the United States—nearly *ninety percent* of the overall market.[40] The largest of these brewers—Anheuser-Busch and MillerCoors—produce *well over* **100 million barrels** of beer each year combined. Jim Koch, founder of the Boston Beer Company (makers of the Samuel Adams line of beer), famously said that, "the big guys [macrobreweries] spill more beer than we make."[41] While that might no longer be true for *his* brewery (the Boston Beer Company produces several million barrels of beer annually), it undoubtedly applies to the majority of craft breweries in the United States.

Many of the most popular beers produced by macrobreweries are at once ubiquitous and uniform. They are brewed both for mass distribution and mass consumption. Almost all of the most popular ones are considered either Light Lagers or American Adjunct Lagers (AAL) initially styled after traditional German or Czech pilsner beers. While once modeled after the source European styles of beer, the modern AAL has changed considerably through the inclusion of brewing adjuncts. It is the addition of these ingredients that gives the beer its classification and also creates the divisive flavor profile common to the style.

Many fans of craft beer hold the brewing process of the larger breweries in disdain because of their heavy reliance on these adjuncts, principally corn and rice. Originally, the substitution of these ingredients for a portion of the malt bill allowed for the brewing of a lighter-bodied, longer-lasting beer that suited the changing tastes of consumers.[42] The fact that the lower prices of corn and rice helped brewers to save on their production costs inspired some to increase their proportion essentially thinning out the beer and making what many feel is a watered-down product as compared with traditional lagers.

Macrobreweries have owned the lion's share of both the American and global beer markets for decades but craft beer has recently impacted their sales figures. The increase in interest in smaller breweries as well as consumers' willingness to spend more money on craft beer has caused these larger breweries to take action. Some have resorted simply to purchasing popular breweries such as Chicago's Goose Island and Seattle's Elysian Brewing while others have heavily increased their marketing presence with various campaigns aimed at drawing consumers back to their well-established brands. Though these beers still dominate the majority of tap handles at bars and restaurants, craft beer continues to expand in popularity and shows no signs of slowing down in the near future.

WHY CHOOSE CRAFT BEER?

I believe that every beer has a place at the table even if I am not a particular fan of a given brand or style. Macrobrewed beer is undeniably more affordable than its craft counterparts and is generally lower in alcohol content. It is therefore perfectly designed for mass consumption: something cold and wet that can give you a buzz given the right quantity; it is simple, straightforward, and unassuming in what it offers.

Craft beer in contrast is enjoyed precisely for its variety and complexity; an embarrassment of riches exists in the craft beer realm for fans of flavor diversity. From potent hop bombs to the deepest, darkest stouts, craft beer offers something for everyone covering multiple drinking philosophies. There are low alcohol beers that allow for greater consumption without sacrificing flavor or quality and extremely high alcohol ones that can be savored more like fine spirits than beer. Some work great as cooking ingredients while others are worthy of having entire meals designed around them.

More than merely enjoyable alcoholic beverages, craft beer represents a *community*—a collection of individuals united by their shared love of innovative breweries and the beers they make. Each brewery has its own unique identity, known as much for its people and philosophies as for its products. Some focus on being rebellious—brewing beers that go against the grain in both their imagery and composition. Others promote a spirit of fun-loving camaraderie while others still emphasize the importance of their locality and honor the history of where they brew.

Simply put, the craft beer community continues to expand because of an openness and willingness to try something new. People who explore craft beer for the first time, whether by visiting their local brewery or simply plucking bottles off of a shelf, are in for an awakening—a moment of transformative taste bud titillation unlike anything they've experienced before.

HOW TO EXPLORE CRAFT BEER

Part of the purpose of this book is to serve as a gateway for the curious or newly initiated craft beer fan. It can be admittedly intimidating to explore something new—especially when it's a world as complex as craft beer. Unfamiliar lingo coupled with seemingly strange beer terms and styles can make someone feel foolish and thus reticent to ask questions about what's on tap. With a lexicon all its own, craft beer can seem incomprehensible especially for someone used to ordering a pint or bottle of the many fizzy yellow options at a local bar. To help assuage those concerns and decipher the terminology, let's explore some of the more common phrases and acronyms.

Whether you're at a craft beer bar, a brewpub, or a brewery, you're likely to encounter a wealth of information about the beer that's available. One of the first things you might notice is the variety of pour sizes available. While most macrobrewed beer comes in bottles or is poured into pint glasses, craft beer is served in a number of ways. Larger pours are quite common—usually sixteen ounces but occasionally twenty ounces or more depending upon the glass size—but smaller pours and different glassware are arguably even more popular.

Most breweries and brewpubs offer samplers or "flights" of their beers. These generally consist of small glasses—typically three to five ounces though occasionally larger—and offer the best opportunity to try a wide variety of beers at one time. Some locations offer predetermined flights but most allow you to choose your own samples from the tap list. Individual samples or tasters are usually available as well at varying but ordinarily nominal costs.

Depending upon the beer, other sizes might be available as well. Stronger beers (ones that are higher in alcohol) might be served in a 9 oz snifter or tulip glass while others, depending upon their style, might have specific glassware associated with them. While this might be viewed as frivolous or unnecessary to the uninitiated, proper glassware plays a pivotal role in both how a beer is perceived and ultimately how it is enjoyed.

Different types of glassware serve different purposes often accentuating a particular quality of the beer. A pilsner glass for example is often used for lagers as its shape helps to retain the beer's head and carbonation. Snifters (not unlike those used for fine spirits) capture and focus the beer's scent or aromatic volatiles, particularly with stronger, more complex brews. Others are used simply for aesthetic purposes either in their own right or because they serve to enhance the beer's appearance.

BEER TERMS

We are a nation that loves acronyms and abbreviations and craft beer is rife with them. Staring at the beer menu, you may question just what the hell it is that you're looking at. While some of the information is superfluous at best much of it *is* important to understanding the beer that you're about to enjoy. On a printed menu you might have the benefit of a written blurb or explanation about the beer but that can tell you only so much; this is where the abbreviations come into play.

Arguably the most important one, ABV stands for "alcohol by volume," and is an indicator of the alcoholic potency of the beer. It is unaffected by the style of the beer, its color, its bitterness, or any other criterion; a 5% abv yellow, hoppy IPA is as exactly as strong as a 5% abv black, sweet milk stout. Most craft beer falls between 4% and 7% though there are a number of much stronger brews that approach and exceed 10%. Though less common, there are some lower alcohol beers that are between 2% and 3%.

The next most critical abbreviation is IBU or "International Bitterness Units." This is an indicator of how bitter a beer is but not necessarily how bitter it *tastes*. As noted earlier, a beer's bitterness is a factor of the alpha acids in the hops and their isomerization during brewing. Consequently, a lower IBU beer will be less bitter than a higher one but just how bitter it is perceived to be can be affected by the other ingredients in the beer. The grain bill or collection of adjuncts can mask or enhance the bitterness of the beer as can an individual's palate sensitivity. As a general guideline though, a beer's IBU number serves as an indicator of whether the beer will taste more or less bitter.

The third most common abbreviation is one that I find to be relatively unnecessary for the average craft beer drinker. SRM or "Standard Reference Method" is a number that describes a beer's color or degree of darkness. Lower, single-digit values lean towards the yellower, clearer end of the spectrum while mid-range numbers through the teens to low-twenties indicate beers that are orange or brown in color. The highest numbers, generally the thirties and above, grow ever darker approaching pitch black.

SRM is useful to a degree. The majority of beers in a given style *will* look similar, meaning that most stouts and porters are dark while most IPAs and hefeweizens are light, for example. The problem though is that there can be a *huge* amount of variation between beers of the same style even though they might have identical SRM values. Some IPAs are extremely hoppy and bitter while others are citrusy and floral; some stouts are smooth and roasty while others taste like a mouthful of coffee or bourbon depending upon the adjuncts used in their brewing.

There is a common misconception that lighter-colored beers taste one way and darker colored beers another. In fact, some people go so far as to avoid beers altogether based solely upon their level of darkness citing that dark brown or black beers are too burnt tasting or too "heavy." Beer styles *do* generally adhere to a certain appearance but with so much variation in flavor and ingredients in craft beer the color does little to add anything meaningful about the individual beer's flavor and should serve merely as a rough guideline.

FINDING YOUR STYLE

Craft beer offers immense variety when it comes to beer styles. Even *within* a given style there can be an impressive spectrum of diversity from one beer to the next. The best way to find what types of styles you enjoy (and don't enjoy!) really is to try as many different beers as you can. One bad batch of a given beer can potentially turn off a drinker not just to that particular brew but to its entire *style*…but it doesn't have to be that way. In fact, it *shouldn't* be that way—not with all that there is to offer within the world of craft beer.

The first rule of thumb to finding your beer style is simply to be open-minded, particularly at the onset. Beer in general is famously touted as being an acquired taste but it is especially true with craft beer because of the sheer intensity of flavors that can be encountered. Your first sip of a 100 IBU India Pale Ale might taste like the most vile, disgusting thing you've ever had in your life but your hundredth sip will likely be beautiful bitter bliss.

Initially, your taste buds experience sensory overload and tend to focus on the most egregious, potent aspects of the beer. Over time and through many encounters, your taste buds and brain build up a sort of memory and gradually filter out the less pleasant aspects allowing the beer's true delicious nature to shine through. I remember thinking when I was younger that Guinness looked like it would taste silky and creamy almost like a beer milkshake; then I had my first sip and it felt like I had licked an ashtray. The reason why was simple: I had never tasted anything like that before. By my third or fourth encounter with the stout, that burnt quality faded away and suddenly I became aware of the sweet, decadent nuances and I was hooked; had I simply grimaced and turned away after that first off-putting sip, I never would have evolved as a beer drinker and I wouldn't have fallen in love with one of my favorite beers!

The second rule of thumb then is to explore a wide variety of beers within a given style, trying individual examples multiple times. If you're turned off by the bitterness of American Pale Ales or India Pale Ales then you might want to start off with something less hoppy and bitter just to prime your taste buds. What I would *not* recommend though is staying in the shallow end of the IBU pool. If you do then you run the risk of stagnating your palate evolution and will wind up sticking to a very narrow scope of beers. Instead, I advocate diving right into the deep end: try the biggest, bitterest, most monstrous mastodon of an IPA—a true hop bomb that will annihilate your taste buds. It might go down as the most offensive thing ever to pass your lips but I can guarantee you that it will serve a greater purpose. After drinking that beer (not just a sip, mind you!), go back and try some of the lower IBU beers. All of a sudden, what you once thought of as bitter and unappealing might magically transform before your very tongue.

Over time, I found that repeat exposure to the most extreme examples of styles rendered my taste buds immune to the most acrimonious, unpalatable aspects and has served to give me a deeper appreciation for the tamer brews among them. There is no reason that you cannot have the same type of experience as long as you approach your craft beer exploration with an open mind and a dedication to broadening your drinking horizons. Be sure to mix it up rather than play it safe—you'll come away with a much better portfolio of beers under your belt and likely a deeper and expanded appreciation not just for *those* beers and styles but for others as well.

STYLE STARTING POINTS

In the face of so many options it can be difficult to know where to begin. This is where flights and samplers come in, giving you the opportunity to dive into multiple styles simultaneously without forcing you to commit to an entire pint of beer. Of course, understanding the difference between beer styles and what you can expect from each one will aid you in your craft beer exploration; understanding your *own* preferences will prove to be even more beneficial.

An easy way to start is simply to find beers that have other things that you like in them. Fruit beers often serve as an entry point for many craft beer converts. The number one reason why most people are reticent to try craft beer is that they are afraid that it will "taste like beer" (meaning, quite often, the ubiquitous macrobrews). Fortunately, and much to the surprise of those individuals, most fruit beers taste nothing like what they think of as beer and are found to be quite palatable from the very first sip.

Coffee is another great adjunct to seek out for first-time beer drinkers. Many stouts and porters are brewed with coffee as an ingredient, which can serve as a bridge between many people's favorite morning beverage and perhaps their new favorite afternoon or evening one. Some beers simply have java characteristics while others taste like a mouthful of iced coffee. Either way, such a beer affords the neophyte craft beer fan the opportunity to form those ever-important nascent taste memories.

I think of beer styles as being similar to music genres and individual breweries being akin to bands: some people limit themselves to only a few genres and groups while others enjoy broader horizons. No one style is better than another—they simply suit your tastes or they don't. As a musician, I am a huge advocate for exploring as many different types of music as possible because there is something profoundly useful to be gained whether you wind up liking them or not. My playing and songwriting are ultimately influenced by my exposure to new things: if I stick only to what I am familiar with then my music becomes boring and repetitive; the same goes for my palate when it comes to beer.

The obvious benefit of trying new or unfamiliar styles of beer is that you might come away with a new favorite; at worst though you will gain a deeper understanding of why you like what you do.

THE STYLES

At the most basic level, craft beers range between being hoppy and bitter to malty and roasted. Along the way you'll encounter beers that are floral or citrusy, fruity or sticky-sweet, crisp and lager-like, mouth-puckeringly tart, and even laden with sour barnyard funk. Not all styles are enjoyed equally and that's fine but they're all equally worthy of exploration.

For the sake of ease and consistency, I will be referencing BeerAdvocate's list of styles as that is the one that I use for my own documentation. There is no single official source of information for beer styles nor is there one to govern the applicability of a given style to a given beer. At times, a single beer might fall under the umbrella of several styles and even then a particular brewer might apply a label that doesn't exist or one that is technically incorrect. In short, styles are important but at times must be used merely as a starting point for describing a beer.

BeerAdvocate's list of styles exceeds <u>one hundred</u> in number and even then fails to capture *every* style I've encountered. There are American India Pale Ales (IPAs) and American Double / Imperial IPAs but no such thing (officially) as a Triple IPA. This supposed style has grown prevalent among brewers as consumer tastes have shifted towards the exceedingly hoppy and bitter. Rather than enjoying its own designation (along with the even rarer Quadruple IPA), it falls under the category of Imperial IPA.

With that said, and with brevity in mind, we will explore the basics of styles separated by flavor profile. It goes without saying that if an American IPA is hoppy and bitter then a Double, Triple, Quadruple, or beyond IPA will be only *more* hoppy and bitter. Certain styles will straddle multiple characteristics while others might fall entirely in between them. In those instances, I will use my own discretion to denote what I believe is the dominant aspect.

*(Please note that the personal recommendations proffered in the section ahead may not all be equally accessible. Some are constrained by geographic distribution, others are restricted by time or season, and others still are extremely limited releases that require some luck to obtain. Beers marked with an asterisk * are exceedingly difficult to obtain either because of limited distribution or availability.)*

LAGERS

The hallmark of most lagers is their clean, crisp taste. Many are European in origin while a few hail from the United States. When people discuss the general flavor of "regular" beer they are likely thinking of a lager.

Pilsener (or Pilsner)

Pilseners are typically Czech or German in origin and feature similar characteristics between the two. They are light in color and flavor and are typically hopped with European varietals called Noble hops. These varieties exhibit a spicy, floral, or even grassy aroma and taste but do not come across as acerbically bitter. They are easy drinking beers that are lower in alcohol—typically between 4% and 6% abv.

COLOR: Light Yellow ALCOHOL: Low SWEETNESS: Low BITTERNESS: Low HOPPINESS: Medium MALTINESS: Low

Widely Available Examples: Pilsner Urquell (Czech Pilsener) and Bitburger Premium Pils (German Pilsener)

My Personal Picks: Russian River STS Pils and Samuel Adams Noble Pils (Czech Pilseners) Sixpoint The Crisp and Victory Prima Pils (German Pilseners)

Euro Pale Lager

Euro Pale Lagers are easily thought of as the European counterpart to the American Adjunct Lager. They are ubiquitous but not unique often embodying an easy-drinking flavor spectrum that is slightly sweet, crisp, and faintly hoppy. These too are between 4% and 6% abv.

COLOR: Light Yellow ALCOHOL: Low SWEETNESS: Low to Medium BITTERNESS: Low HOPPINESS: Low to Medium MALTINESS: Low

Widely Available Examples: Stella Artois and Heineken Lager Beer

My Personal Picks: Samuel Smith's Organically Produced Lager Beer and Guinness Harp Lager

Vienna Lager

Vienna Lagers are typically slightly darker in color and sweeter than other lager style beers. Their alcohol content occasionally dips below 4% and above 6% but falls again in the typical range. This is an excellent starting point for folks who enjoy sweeter beers and who find the trademark lager-taste palatable.

COLOR: Darker Yellow to Light Amber ALCOHOL: Low SWEETNESS: Medium BITTERNESS: Low HOPPINESS: Low MALTINESS: Medium

Widely Available Examples: Samuel Adams Boston Lager and Dos Equis Amber Lager

My Personal Picks: Samuel Adams Boston Lager, Great Lakes Eliot Ness, and Blue Point Toasted Lager

Märzen / Oktoberfest

Perhaps one of the most well-known styles, Oktoberfest beers are available in the late summer through early winter. They are darker, often copper or amber in color, fuller-bodied than other lighter lagers, richer and sweeter in flavor with an occasionally toasted aspect, and are usually higher in alcohol, typically between 5% and 7%. They are smooth and pair well with a variety of foods making them among the most versatile beers. This is one of my favorite styles and is one that I favored heavily early on in my craft beer exploration.

COLOR: Between Amber and Copper ALCOHOL: Medium SWEETNESS: Medium to High BITTERNESS: Low HOPPINESS: Low MALTINESS: Medium to High

Widely Available Examples: Samuel Adams Octoberfest, Sierra Nevada Oktoberfest

My Personal Picks: Ramstein Oktoberfest, Great Lakes Oktoberfest, Spaten Oktoberfestbier Ur-Märzen, Ayinger Oktober Fest-Märzen, and Paulaner Oktoberfest-Märzen

Bock / Doppelbock

Bocks and Doppelbocks are among the strongest, darkest, and maltiest lagers. They are typically enjoyed during the colder months when heartier beers are often preferred over their lighter-bodied brethren. The flavor of Bock beers is far more potent than the other styles and may be off-putting at first but the malt profile often balances the alcoholic punch and occasionally bitter hop profile. Single Bocks typically fall between 5%-7% while Doppelbocks (or "double" bocks) regularly approach 9% and often embody a more roasted aspect.

COLOR: Dark Amber to Black ALCOHOL: Medium to High SWEETNESS: Medium BITTERNESS: Medium HOPPINESS: Low MALTINESS: High

Widely Available Examples: Shiner Bock, Ayinger Celebrator Doppelbock, and Spaten Optimator

My Personal Picks: Samuel Adams Winter Lager, Ayinger Celebrator Doppelbock, Spaten Optimator, Samichlaus Classic Bier, Smuttynose S'muttonator, and Urbock 23°

Rauchbier

Rauchbier is arguably the most challenging lager style to get into. It is similar to Oktoberfest beers in its composition but it is made with smoked malts that produce intense and potentially off-putting flavors. These aspects are often described as tasting like bacon, tobacco, leather, and smoked meats like ham and sausage. Many people enjoy the beer alongside smoked meats but for me the combination is overpowering. This is not a style I particularly enjoy but one that I encourage everyone to try at least once just to see how different beer can taste.

COLOR: Amber to Dark Brown ALCOHOL: Medium to High SWEETNESS: Medium BITTERNESS: Low HOPPINESS: Low MALTINESS: Medium (SMOKINESS: SUPER HIGH!)

Widely Available Examples: Aecht Schlenkerla Rauchbier Märzen and Samuel Adams Cinder Bock*

My Personal Picks: Aecht Schlenkerla Rauchbier Urbock

ALES

Ale styles represent both the majority of beer types and the broadest variety. Like lagers, most hail from the United States, England, and Germany but a fair number come from Belgium, France, Scotland, and Ireland. Ales run the gamut of hoppiness, bitterness, sweetness, sourness, maltiness, roastiness, and fruitiness and as such are difficult to describe with broad strokes. Instead, we'll begin with the styles that are the easiest to get into and work our way up to the boldest, most intense ones that beer has to offer.

EASY DRINKING / SEASONALS

German Altbier

Altbier is a type of brown ale that is balanced in its malty sweetness and hop character. It is average in alcohol content and smooth drinking, which makes this an ideal entry point for craft beer fans. Altbiers are often found in the spring either as a brewery's seasonal release or as a complement to one.

COLOR: Amber to Dark Brown ALCOHOL: Medium SWEETNESS: Medium BITTERNESS: Low HOPPINESS: Medium MALTINESS: Medium FRUITINESS: Low

Widely Available Examples: Long Trail Ale

My Personal Picks: Alaskan Amber* and Long Trail Double Bag

American Blonde Ale

American Blonde Ales are among my personal favorites for introducing friends to craft beer. They are light bodied, slightly malty, subtly fruity, and lower in alcohol, which makes them instantly accessible to any palate. Often golden in color, they are reminiscent of silken shores and sun-kissed sand—fitting as many breweries offer this style as their summer seasonal beer!

COLOR: Light Yellow to Golden ALCOHOL: Low to Medium SWEETNESS: Medium BITTERNESS: Low HOPPINESS: Low to Medium MALTINESS: Medium FRUITINESS: Low to Medium

Widely Available Examples: Victory Brewing Summer Love and Deschutes River Ale

My Personal Picks: The Bruery Or Xata*, Kona Brewing Big Wave Golden Ale, Flying Fish Farmhouse Summer Ale, New Belgium Brewing Somersault, Narragansett Summer Ale

Cream Ale

Cream ales are known primarily for their sweet, creamy texture. These are light in color, bitterness, body, and flavor— perfect warm-weather beers to quench one's thirst. They pair well with almost any food and serve as perfect palate primers for craft beer newcomers!

COLOR: Light Yellow to Golden ALCOHOL: Medium SWEETNESS: Medium BITTERNESS: Low HOPPINESS: Low MALTINESS: Medium FRUITINESS: Low

Widely Available Examples: Anderson Valley Summer Solstice, New Glarus Spotted Cow, Climax Cream Ale

My Personal Picks: Carton Regular Coffee*, Sixpoint Sweet Action, Ballast Point Calm Before The Storm

Kölsch

Kölsch is one of my favorite styles of beer because of how crisp and dry it tastes despite not being a lager. It tends to be a little more bitter compared with the other beers in the easy drinking category but I don't believe that it is enough to be off-putting. It is also one of the few beer styles that is directly linked to a particular region—in this case Cologne, Germany. This is the only place in the world where authentic Kölsch beer is made; if it's made anywhere else then it's merely considered to be Kölsch-style beer.[43]

COLOR: Pale Yellow to Light Gold ALCOHOL: Medium SWEETNESS: Medium BITTERNESS: Medium HOPPINESS: Low to Medium MALTINESS: Low to Medium FRUITINESS: Low to Medium

Widely Available Examples: Rock Bottom Brewery Kolsch, Harpoon Summer Beer, Schlafly Kölsch

My Personal Picks: Captain Lawrence Captain's Kölsch, Alaskan Summer Ale*

American Amber / Red Ale

Arguably the single most ubiquitous style of beer among brewpub offerings, the Amber or Red Ale is seemingly on every beer menu I've encountered. It is among the sweetest and maltiest of the easy drinking beers and often embodies fainter hop profiles along with muted fruitiness typical of ales. It serves as an excellent segue to other bolder styles and is worth exploration by any beer fan.

COLOR: Amber to Red ALCOHOL: Medium

SWEETNESS: Medium to High BITTERNESS: Low to Medium

HOPPINESS: Low MALTINESS: Medium to High FRUITINESS: Medium

Widely Available Examples: New Belgium Fat Tire Amber Ale, Stone Brewing Levitation Ale, Great Lakes Nosferatu, Bell's Amber Ale, Lagunitas Censored

My Personal Picks: Maine Brewing Company's Zoe, Maine Brewing Company's Red Wheelbarrow, Cigar City Tocobaga, Sierra Nevada Flipside Red IPA

Fruit Beers

Fruit beer is a catchall category that consists primarily of brews that are made either with real fruit or with an adjunct or extract that provides the desired fruit flavor or quality. The fruit aspect typically dominates the beer's flavor and aroma dampening whatever malt and hop qualities exist. Outside of the American Blonde Ale and American Amber / Red Ale, Fruit Beers seem to be the single most popular conversion point for non-beer drinkers on their journey to craft beer nirvana. Many an imbiber has claimed that they despise beer only to find him- or herself enamored with the sweet, rich flavor of a fruit beer. The inevitable expression of awe is often accompanied by a proclamation such as, "I had no idea that *beer* could taste like *this*!"

I recommend fruit beers for the most reticent of drinkers if for nothing other than the fact that it opens their minds and preps their palates to craft beer. They are also a fine way of bridging the gap for fans of fruitier wine styles.

COLOR: Varies ALCOHOL: Varies SWEETNESS: Varies but typically High BITTERNESS: Low HOPPINESS: Low MALTINESS: Low to Medium FRUITINESS: Highest

Widely Available Examples: Magic Hat #9, Leinenkugel's Summer Shandy, Abita Brewing Purple Haze, 21st Amendment Hell Or High Watermelon Wheat, Samuel Adams Cherry Wheat, Sea Dog Blueberry Wheat Ale, Samuel Smith Organic Fruit Beers

My Personal Picks:

RASPBERRY New Glarus Raspberry Tart, Founders Rübæus (or Blushing Monk—a more potent version), Dogfish Head Fort*

CHERRY Founders Cerise

APPLE Unibroue Éphémère (Apple)

BLUEBERRY Dogfish Head Black & Blue, Blue Point Blueberry

STRAWBERRY New Glarus Strawberry Rhubarb

PEACH RJ Rockers Son Of A Peach, Spellbound Peach IPA

APRICOT Dogfish Head Aprihop IPA (very hoppy and bitter!), Pyramid Apricot Ale

LEMON Curious Traveler Lemon Shandy

PASSION FRUIT Kona Brewing Wailua Wheat, Avery Liliko'I Kepolo

WATERMELON 21st Amendment Hell Or High Watermelon Wheat Beer

COCONUT Oskar Blues Death By Coconut*, Maui CoCoNut Porter*

BANANA Well's Banana Bread Beer

MANGO Minneapolis Town Hall Mango Mama, Spellbound Mango IPA

SPICED BEERS

While malts and hops tend to dominate the beer flavor profile other more exotic tastes can often be encountered, particularly spices. Certain styles embody a literal potpourri of ingredients that provide a unique medley of aromas and tastes. These types of beers are often hit-or-miss depending upon the drinker's preferences but should be experienced nonetheless. Here are four styles that embody a certain degree of seasonality pairing perfectly with their respective times of year.

Witbier

The Belgian witbier is the perfect late-winter/springtime beer given its crisp, tangy sweetness, its ebullient carbonation, and its mélange of spices. Herbaceous in their bouquets, witbiers are typically spiced with coriander and orange peel and occasionally imbued with other culinary herbs and spices. Witbiers are often served with a lemon slice or wedge, which brightens the beer considerably but serves also to eradicate the finer nuances of the spices. The wheat in the grain bill provides a spicy twang that complements the aforementioned adjuncts nicely.

COLOR: Cloudy, Pale Yellow ALCOHOL: Medium SWEETNESS: Medium to High BITTERNESS: Low HOPPINESS: Low MALTINESS: Low FRUITINESS: Medium SPICE LEVEL: Medium to High

Widely Available Examples: Hoegaarden Original White Ale, Harpoon UFO White

My Personal Picks: Allagash White, Dogfish Head Namaste

Hefeweizen

Hefeweizens are excellent year-round beers that shine the brightest during the spring and summer. This is a relatively ubiquitous style among brewpubs throughout the United States and often graces the beer menus of breweries during the aforementioned seasons. Among the more distinct styles of beer, hefeweizens almost universally exhibit aroma notes and flavors of banana and cloves derived from the esters produced during fermentation; bubblegum aromas are also encountered occasionally. Once again, lemons are often served as a flavor-enhancing garnish although they are sometimes replaced with orange wedges.

COLOR: Hazy Yellow ALCOHOL: Medium SWEETNESS: Medium BITTERNESS: Low HOPPINESS: Low MALTINESS: Low to Medium FRUITINESS: Medium SPICE LEVEL: Medium

Widely Available Examples: Sierra Nevada Kellerweis Hefeweizen

My Personal Picks: Weihenstephaner Hefeweissbier, Franziskaner Hefe-Weisse

Winter Warmer

As its name implies, the winter warmer style of beer pairs perfectly with a warm fire on a cold winter's night. Rich, dark, and often heavily spiced with classic wintertime spices like ginger, cinnamon, nutmeg, star anise, and cardamom, winter warmers evoke the sights and smells of the holidays. When crafted properly, they taste like Christmas in a glass but, if overly or improperly spiced, they can be terrible, one-note messes. Some winter warmers are not spiced at all and would be better sought out by those who prefer a less earthy brew.

COLOR: Deep Copper to Dark Black ALCOHOL: Medium to High SWEETNESS: Medium BITTERNESS: Low HOPPINESS: Low MALTINESS: Medium to High FRUITINESS: Low to Medium SPICE LEVEL: High (if spiced)

Widely Available Examples: Samuel Smith's Winter Welcome Ale, Anchor Brewing Our Special Ale

My Personal Picks: Samuel Adams Old Fezziwig Ale (*tastes like a Christmas cookie in a glass!*), Philadelphia Brewing Company Winter Wünder

Pumpkin Ales

The humble pumpkin ale has become one of the most polarizing styles in all of craft beer. It is almost exclusively beloved or reviled by craft drinkers because of its meteoric rise in popularity. Once exclusively autumnal offerings, pumpkin ales have become arguably the most egregious exemplar of seasonal creep now appearing on shelves as early as August. Some pumpkin ales are faint in their pumpkin essence and are quite similar to Märzens/Oktoberfests in their maltiness while others exist as liquid pumpkin pie in a glass. The tamer examples offer faint pumpkin sweetness while others are unabashed spice bombs with overwhelming doses of pumpkin pie spices like nutmeg, cinnamon, allspice, and ginger.

When offered on draft, pumpkin ales are occasionally served in a pint glass with a cinnamon sugar rim. _Many_ a beer drinker conversion has occurred with such a setup including my wife who fell in love with John Harvard's Pumpkin Spice.

COLOR: Light Copper to Dark Amber ALCOHOL: Medium SWEETNESS: Medium to High BITTERNESS: Low HOPPINESS: Low MALTINESS: Medium to High FRUITINESS: Low to Medium SPICE LEVEL: High (if spiced)

Widely Available Examples: Southern Tier Pumking, Dogfish Head Punkin Ale

My Personal Picks: Southern Tier Pumking, Dogfish Head Punkin Ale, Schlafly Pumpkin Ale

Bonus Picks: Heavy Seas Great'ER Pumpkin* (*Bourbon Barrel Aged*), Avery Rumpkin* and Pump[KY]n* (*Rum Barrel and Bourbon Barrel Aged, respectively*)

STRONGER STYLES

While the styles we've just explored represent excellent entry points they barely scratch the surface of what craft beer can offer. When thinking of one's palate, I find myself often comparing its development to level building in a role playing game like Final Fantasy. Early on, you don't have much experience and if you venture too far into areas filled with stronger creatures (or stronger beers, in this case), then you risk being overwhelmed and ultimately disheartened. Take the time to *build up* that experience through encounters with tamer foes (or brews) and over time you become readier for the bigger challenges; these, in turn, ultimately offer the greatest reward for your efforts.

There are a number of styles that are typically more bombastic and thus less approachable than the ones that have already been outlined. For sake of ease, I will group them into four categories: malt-forward, hop-forward, Belgian, and sour. This way, once you've identified your palate's proclivities, you can dive directly into the group that you're most interested in before exploring the others.

STRONG MALT-FORWARD

The beers comprising this category all tend to be malt-heavy with hops and bitterness contributing little to their flavors and aromas. Whereas the previous malt-forward beers tended to be more on the sweeter side, the brews in this section broaden the spectrum and include heavier roast levels, thicker bodies, and ordinarily higher alcohol content than the others.

Brown Ale

I think of brown ales as being graduated red ales. They tend to be just as malty and sweet as their amber associates but are simultaneously far more rich and complex. Brown ales are typically English or American in origin with, at least for me, a notable difference in the drinking experience between the two. English brown ales tend to be thinner in their mouthfeel, sweeter, and either nuttier or fruitier in their flavor. American brown ales tend to be bolder, fuller in their mouthfeel, maltier and oftentimes more roasted in their flavor. Maple syrup and coffee are two common adjuncts that are often added to this style.

(Author's note: between English and American versions of the same beer style, I usually gravitate more towards the American ones because they are usually bolder and broader in terms of their flavors. By contrast, I find the English styles to be milder and occasionally watered down. This might however be preferable to some so I encourage you to try examples of both to see which you enjoy more.)

COLOR: Light and Ruddy to Deep, Dark Brown

ALCOHOL: Medium to High SWEETNESS: Medium

BITTERNESS: Low HOPPINESS: Low MALTINESS: Medium to High FRUITINESS: Medium ROAST: Medium

Widely Available Examples (*English Brown Ale*): Newcastle Brown Ale, Samuel Smith's Nut Brown Ale, Abita Brewing Turbodog

(*American Brown Ale*): Big Sky Brewing's Moose Drool Brown Ale, Avery Brewing's Ellie's Brown Ale

My Personal Picks (*English Brown Ale*): Milwaukee Ale House's Block Head Brown, Belford Brewing's Lobster Pot Ale, 16 Mile Brewing Company Harvest Ale, Lazy Magnolia's Southern Pecan

(*American Brown Ale*): Flossmoor Station's Pullman Brown Ale, Captain Lawrence Brown Bird Brown Ale, Dogfish Head's Palo Santo Marron (*aged on Palo Santo wood*), Spellbound Brewing's Gingerbread Brown, Dogfish Head's Indian Brown Ale (*hoppy like an IPA*), Surly Coffee Bender* (*HUGE coffee presence*)

Scotch Ale / Wee Heavy

Scotch ales are strong, sweet beers that have a pleasant, potent roasted caramel aspect. As easy drinking as they are alcoholic, scotch ales bear bourbon barrel aging well, creating a delectable marriage between the oak and vanilla overtones of the barrel with their already sweet caramel qualities. The alternate name Wee Heavy is derived from a time when Scottish beers were dubbed based upon the shilling currency.

Scotch ales serve as an excellent precursor to barleywines and are among my favorite styles of beer.

COLOR: Amber, Copper, and Light Brown ALCOHOL: Medium to High SWEETNESS: Medium to High BITTERNESS: Low HOPPINESS: Low MALTINESS: Medium to High FRUITINESS: Low to Medium ROAST: Medium

Widely Available Examples: Oskar Blues Old Chub – Scottish Style Ale, Founders Dirty Bastard, Orkney SkullSplitter, Smuttynose Scotch Style Ale (Big Beer Series)

My Personal Picks: Founders Backwoods Bastard*, Thirsty Dog Wulver*, Fordham Brewing Scotch Ale, Philadelphia Brewing Company Kilty Pleasure, AleSmith Wee Heavy

Porter

Porter is one of the longest-lasting beer styles deriving an origin from at least the 1700s if not earlier. According to BeerAdvocate's beer style page, "Porter was a blend of three different styles: an old ale (stale or soured), a new ale (brown or pale ale) and a weak one (mild ale), with various combinations of blending and staleness…It was the first truly engineered beer, catering to the public's taste, playing a critical role in…building the mega-breweries of today."[44] Centuries later, it still remains among the most popular styles in the world.

To me, porters bridge the gap between brown ales and stouts: they are slightly sweet and complex like the former but begin to delve into the dark, roasted depths of the latter. Porters also cater well to adjuncts like coffee and barrel aging, particularly in whiskey barrels. Once more, there is a distinct difference between American and European designations. English porters, again, tend to be lighter-bodied, less roasted and malt-dominant, but still complex. American porters are fuller flavored, tend towards a heavier, more roasted mouthfeel, and often employ the inclusion of adjuncts like vanilla, chocolate, and coffee or the use of smoked malts.

Baltic porter is a third branch of the style and is also English in origin. *This* style though is by far the most potent of the three. It was designed to survive trips across the North Sea and was thus brewed to be bolder and more robust by nature. Personally, for as much as I enjoy and appreciate big, bold beers, I've yet to fall in love with the Baltic porter style even though the few that I have had have been excellent.

COLOR: Dark Brown to Deep Black ALCOHOL: Medium to High SWEETNESS: Medium BITTERNESS: Low HOPPINESS: Low MALTINESS: Medium FRUITINESS: Low ROAST: Medium to High

Widely Available Examples (*English Porter*): Fuller's London Porter, Samuel Smith's The Famous Taddy Porter, Meantime London Porter

(*American Porter*): Anchor Porter, Sierra Nevada Porter, Samuel Adams Holiday Porter

(*Baltic Porter*): Smuttynose Baltic Porter, Baltika #6 Porter, Victory Baltic Thunder

My Personal Picks (*English Porter*): Harviestoun Old Engine Oil, Yards Brewing's General Washington's Tavern Porter

(*American Porter*): Hill Farmstead Everett Porter* (*hands down the best regular porter I've ever tasted*), Great Lakes Edmund Fitzgerald Porter (*a close second to Everett*), Deschutes Black Butte Porter, Founders Porter, Evil Twin Lil' B, Kona Pipeline Porter, Alaskan Smoked Porter*, Stone Brewing Smoked Porter (*especially the Vanilla Bean variant*), Ballast Point Victory At Sea Coffee Vanilla Imperial Porter*, Evil Twin Imperial Doughnut Break, Kane Brewing Morning Bell*, Sunday Brunch*, or Mexican Brunch* (*porter made with coffee, maple syrup, and cinnamon*)

(*Baltic Porter*): Flying Dog Gonzo Imperial Porter (*also a barrel aged version*), Jack's Abby Framinghammer (*also numerous barrel aged versions*), Sixpoint 4Beans, Arcadia Brewing's Bourbon Barrel Aged Shipwreck Porter

Stout

Along with India Pale Ales, stouts are my favorite types of beer. Stouts tend to be tantalizingly dark, roasted, and bold with some of the imperial versions approaching or exceeding *twenty-percent* abv. People often ask what the difference is between a porter and a stout and the short answer is: very little. Stouts are essentially strong porters and eventually branched off as its own style but technically the difference between them is a semantic one.

With that said, stouts tend to venture further than porters in nearly every category: level of roast, darkness of color, and strength of alcohol to name but three. Though there are weaker, more easy-drinking stouts, the best of the style tend to push the limits and embody unrivaled boldness. For those who like lower-alcohol, smoother, sweeter, and lighter-bodied brews, there are English Stouts, Irish Dry Stouts, Oatmeal Stouts, and Milk or Sweet Stouts to consider; for those looking for richer, more complex brews, there are American Stouts, their Double or Imperial counterparts, Foreign / Export Stouts, and the gargantuan Russian Imperial Stout.

Stouts stand up well to the inclusion of numerous adjuncts like chocolate, coffee, vanilla, chile peppers, coconut, and spices like cinnamon; they also derive arguably the most of any style from extended stays in spirits barrels.

COLOR: Deep Brown to Impenetrable Black ALCOHOL: Medium to Extremely High SWEETNESS: Varies by style but typically Medium to High BITTERNESS: Low HOPPINESS: Low MALTINESS: Medium to High ROASTINESS: Medium to High

Widely Available Examples

(*English Stout*): Yards Brewing Love Stout, Innis & Gunn Bourbon Stout

(*Irish Dry Stout*): Guinness Draught, Murphy's Irish Stout

(*Oatmeal Stout*): Samuel Smith's Oatmeal Stout, Firestone Walker Velvet Merlin, Barney Flats Oatmeal Stout

(*Milk / Sweet Stout*): Young's Double Chocolate Stout, Left Hand Milk Stout

(*Foreign / Export Stout*): Ceylon / Lion Brewing's Lion Stout, Guinness Foreign Extra Stout

(*American Stout*): Bell's Java Stout, Sierra Nevada Stout

(*American Double / Imperial Stout*): Founders Breakfast Stout, New Holland Dragon's Milk, AleSmith Speedway Stout, Great Divide Oatmeal Yeti

(*Russian Imperial Stout*): Stone Russian Imperial Stout, Great Divide Yeti, Founders Imperial Stout, Oskar Blues Ten FIDY

My Personal Picks:

(*English Stout*): Cooperstown Strike Out Stout, Orkney Dragonhead Stout

(*Irish Dry Stout*): Guinness Draught, Guinness Extra Stout, Victory Donnybrook Stout

(*Oatmeal Stout*): Rogue Ales Shakespeare Oatmeal Stout, Firestone Walker Velvet Merkin*, New Holland The Poet, Heartland Brewery Farmer Jon's Oatmeal Stout, Mikkeller Beer Geek Breakfast

(*Milk / Sweet Stout*): Lancaster Milk Stout, Carton Brewing Carton Of Milk, Ormond Brewing The Dude Coffee Milk Stout, Neshaminy Creek Coconut Mudbank Milk Stout, Terrapin Moo-Hoo Chocolate Milk Stout

(*Foreign / Export Stout*): Guinness Foreign Extra Stout, Schlafly Irish-Style Extra Stout

(*American Stout*): Bell's Kalamazoo Stout, Maine Brewing Mean Old Tom, Deschutes Obsidian Stout

(*American Double / Imperial Stout*): Weyerbacher Sunday Morning Stout*, Victory Storm King Stout, Goose Island Night Stalker, Goose Island Big John

(BONUS: The Bruery's Black Tuesday*, Founders KBS (Kentucky Breakfast Stout)*, Goose Island Bourbon County Brand

Stout*, Deschutes The Abyss*--*all incredibly difficult to find but among the best beers I've ever had!*)

(*Russian Imperial Stout*): Firestone Walker Parabola*, Thirsty Dog Siberian Night (both regular and barrel aged), Sierra Nevada Narwhal Imperial Stout, North Coast Old Rasputin Russian Imperial Stout, Bell's Expedition Stout, Weyerbacher Old Heathen or Heresy

Barleywine

Barleywines serve as a bit of a departure point for our journey so far; it's the first truly intense style that will utterly annihilate the unsuspecting palate. Though strong in nearly every aspect, barleywines are also among the most complex and potentially enjoyable styles if approached correctly. The first few might seem like hot messes drenched in alcohol but over time the nuances will shine through allowing the true nature of the beer to be experienced.

Both American and English barleywines exhibit thick, heavy, alcohol-laden bodies and vary widely from sweet, fruity esters to utter hop bombs. Almost exclusively higher in alcohol, barleywines benefit not just from aging but from *warming*; they are one of the few styles that actually morph and improve over time if left to approach room temperature. Strong, dry, not cloyingly sweet, and often imbued with pleasant fruitiness, barleywines are among the pinnacle of craft beer offerings.

COLOR: Varies widely between Dark, Sticky Gold to Deep Amber, Garnet, and Dark Brown. ALCOHOL: High to Extremely High SWEETNESS: Typically High but rarely cloying BITTERNESS: High in some examples HOPPINESS: High in some examples MALTINESS: Medium to High FRUITINESS: Medium to High ROASTINESS: Low

Widely Available Examples

(*English Barleywine*): Anchor Old Foghorn, J.W. Lees Vintage Harvest Ale

(*American Barleywine*): Sierra Nevada Bigfoot Barleywine Style Ale, AleSmith Old Numbskull, Great Divide Old Ruffian Barley Wine, Stone Old Guardian Barley Wine Style Ale

My Personal Picks:

(*English Barleywine*): Firestone Walker Sucaba*, Weyerbacher Insanity and Blithering Idiot, Goose Island Bourbon

County Brand Barleywine Ale*, Avery Brewing Samael's Ale, The Bruery Mash, Pelican Pub & Brewery's Mother Of All Storms

(*American Barleywine*): Sierra Nevada Bigfoot Barleywine Style Ale, Dogfish Head Olde School Barleywine*, Kane Brewing Vengeful Heart, Rogue XS Old Crustacean, Avery Hog Heaven Barley Wine, Uinta Brewing Cockeyed Cooper

Strong Ales

Strong ale is essentially a catch-all term that covers beers that are either hybrid in style or ones that fail to be categorized easily. English Strong Ales are actually less potent than barleywines while American Strong Ales rival them in terms of their alcoholic bite, occasional hoppiness, and fruit qualities. English Strong Ales usually cap off at around 7.5% abv while American Strong Ales tend to *start* at that level of alcohol.

COLOR: Varies widely but usually Darker in color ALCOHOL: Medium for English Strong Ales, High to Extremely High for American ones SWEETNESS: Typically High BITTERNESS: High in some examples HOPPINESS: High in some examples MALTINESS: Typically High FRUITINESS: Medium to High ROASTINESS: Low

Widely Available Examples

(*English Strong Ale*): Wychwood Brewery's King Goblin, Coopers Extra Strong Vintage Ale, Ridgeway Brewing Insanely / Seriously Bad Elf

(*American Strong Ale*): Stone Brewing's Arrogant Bastard / Double Bastard Ale, Lagunitas Brewing's Brown Shugga', Rogue Double Dead Guy Ale, Long Trail Brewing Triple Bag

My Personal Picks:

(*English Strong Ale*): Yards' Thomas Jefferson's Tavern Ale, Cooperstown Brewing's Pride of Milford Strong Malty Ale, Porterhouse Brewing's An Brain Blásta

(*American Strong Ale*): The Lost Abbey's Deliverance Ale and The Angel's Share (Bourbon Barrel Aged), Stone Brewing Oaked Arrogant Bastard Ale, Sierra Nevada Life & Limb

(BONUS: Samuel Adams Utopias (*almost 30% abv!*)*, Firestone Walker Anniversary Ale*, The Bruery's Melange No. 3*-- *again, all difficult to obtain but utterly worth the effort!*)

STRONG BITTER / HOP FORWARD

In my experience I have found that the primary reason that people choose not to drink beer is because they do not like the taste. In most cases, they are referring to macrobrewed beers but on occasion they speak of craft beer as well; the chief complaint in these instances is almost always that the beer was too bitter. Bitterness, much like most qualities of craft beer, is an acquired taste; the more you encounter it, the less offensive it may seem to your palate over time. Eventually, the negative aspects of bitter or hoppy beers will start to fade and you will begin to pick up on the pleasant tastes and aromas that have led millions of craft beer fans to fall in love with India Pale Ales and similar styles.

Any beer can be made bitter or hoppy through the addition of hops (as outlined earlier) however as a general rule none of the styles that we have discussed so far embody any hop-heavy qualities. The ensuing styles though can be nothing short of bitter bombs exploding with hoppiness. These should be approached with the understanding that, if at the onset they prove to be too much, then over time they will become more palatable if given the chance.

Pale Ales

Pale ales are an excellent stepping stone to the more potent India Pale Ale. These beers, while hoppy and bitter, are often fruitier with a stronger malt backbone than their ultra hopped counterparts. English versions tend to be maltier than American ones, which favor more potent hop profiles. Pale ales are often more balanced beers than India Pale Ales and typically lower in alcohol as well.

COLOR: Light Gold to Amber or Copper ALCOHOL: Medium SWEETNESS: Low BITTERNESS: Medium to High HOPPINESS: Medium to High MALTINESS: Medium FRUITINESS: Medium

Widely Available Examples

(*English Pale Ale*): Boddingtons Pub Ale, Bass Pale Ale, Fuller's London Pride

(*American Pale Ale*): Sierra Nevada Pale Ale, Sweetwater 420 Extra Pale Ale

My Personal Picks:

(*English Pale Ale*): Coopers Sparkling Ale, Great Divide Denver Pale Ale, Bass Pale Ale

(*American Pale Ale*): 3 Floyds Brewing Zombie Dust* or Alpha King*, Alpine Beer Company's Hoppy Birthday, Oskar Blue's Dale's Pale Ale, Founders Pale Ale, Maine MO or Peeper Ale

India Pale Ales

India Pale Ales (or IPAs) are the zenith for fans of bitter, hoppy beers. These craft beer lovers called hop heads seek out the highest IBU brews and enjoy the variety of hop profiles from dank and earthen, to fragrantly floral, to tropical and fruity, and ultimately to piney and resinous. These beers tend to be an all-out assault on the senses and can be admittedly overwhelming at the onset; those who press on and continue to explore their ranks however are ultimately (and deliciously!) rewarded for their efforts.

IPAs are typically divided into five categories: English, American, Double or Imperial, Black (also called American Black Ales or Cascadian Dark Ales), and Belgian. Each style features hoppiness and bitterness as its dominant descriptor but the individual intricacies of each style provide for a remarkable and easily identifiable amount of variation. English IPAs tend to be lower in alcohol, more relaxed in bitterness, and slightly more malt-forward rendering them the closest to pale ales of all of the IPA variations.

American IPAs are usually higher in alcohol, more flavorful, maltier, and hoppier than their English contemporaries. Double or Imperial IPAs magnify all of those qualities exponentially creating the bitterest, hoppiest, most potent brews imaginable. Black IPAs are relatively new and feature not merely a darker appearance than others of its ilk but also an amenable marriage to a roastier, malted backbone.

Lastly, Belgian IPAs combine the trademark Belgian yeast flavor with American bitterness sensibility. These tend to be higher in alcohol than the typical English or American IPA, are drier and cleaner, and showcase the distinct Belgian yeast quality that we will explore in a later section.

COLOR: Light Gold to Dark Amber (Dark Brown and Black for Black IPAs) ALCOHOL: Medium to Extremely High SWEETNESS: Low to Medium BITTERNESS: High to Extremely High HOPPINESS: High to Extremely High MALTINESS: Medium (or High for some Black IPAs) FRUITINESS: Medium to High ROASTINESS: Low though Black IPAs are usually Medium

Widely Available Examples

(*English India Pale Ale*): Samuel Smith's India Pale Ale, Flying Fish HopFish IPA, Goose Island India Pale Ale

(*American India Pale Ale*): Firestone Walker Union Jack India Pale Ale, Cigar City Jai Alai IPA, Bell's Two Hearted Ale, Stone IPA, AleSmith IPA

(*American Double / Imperial India Pale Ale*): Dogfish Head 90 Minute IPA, Founders Double Trouble, Green Flash West Coast IPA, Avery Maharaja

(*American Black Ale / Cascadian Dark Ale*): Stone Sublimely Self-Righteous Ale, Southern Tier Iniquity (Imperial Black Ale), Lagunitas NightTime, Founders Dark Penance

(*Belgian India Pale Ale*): Flying Dog Raging Bitch Belgian-Style IPA, Green Flash Le Freak, Clown Shoes Tramp Stamp

My Personal Picks:

(*English India Pale Ale*): Yards India Pale Ale, Goose Island India Pale Ale, Flying Fish HopFish, Great Lakes Commodore Perry IPA

(*American India Pale Ale*): Russian River Blind Pig IPA, The Alchemist Focal Banger*, Kane Head High, Dogfish Head 60

Minute IPA, Fat Head's Head Hunter IPA, Sierra Nevada Torpedo Extra IPA or Celebration Ale, Ballast Point Grapefruit Sculpin, Trillium Melcher Street and Congress Street IPAs

(*American Double / Imperial India Pale Ale*): Russian River Pliny The Elder, Stone Enjoy By IPA, 3 Floyds Brewing Arctic Panzer Wolf, Great Lakes Chillwave Double IPA, Bell's Hopslam Ale, Dogfish Head Burton Baton, Carton Brewing 077XX, Victory Brewing DirtWolf, Founders Devil Dancer*, Surly Abrasive Ale*, Odell Brewing Myrcenary Double IPA, Alpine Brewing Pure Hoppiness, Other Half All Green Everything or Green Diamonds, Knee Deep Brewing Simtra, Neshaminy Creek The Shape Of Hops To Come, Fat Head's Hop JuJu Imperial IPA, Goose Island The Illinois, Kane Brewing Overhead*, Captain Lawrence's Palate Shifter, New England Brewing G-Bot Double IPA and Coriolis

(NOTE: The following are among my favorites but are exceedingly difficult to obtain. Russian River Pliny The Younger, The Alchemist Heady Topper, Dogfish Head 120 Minute IPA)

(*American Black Ale / Cascadian Dark Ale*): Firestone Walker Wookey Jack, Blue Point BP Toxic Sludge, Stone Sublimely

Self-Righteous Ale, Uinta Dubhe Imperial Black IPA, Victory Hop Ticket Black IPA, Otter Creek Alpine Black IPA

(*Belgian India Pale Ale*): Clown Shoes Muffin Top, Lagunitas A Little Sumpin' Wild, Stone Cali-Belgique

BELGIAN BEERS

Belgian beers have been around for centuries and have enjoyed a resurgence resembling a cult following among American craft beer fans in recent years. Great variety exists within the category but the one unifying element among all of the styles is the unmistakable Belgian yeast strain; this is what provides the quintessential fruity, ester-laden flavor unique to the region. Many of the beers are made at monasteries and are thus dubbed "Abbey Beers" while a select few made by those of the Trappist order are called "Trappist Beers"; as of the present moment, there are only eleven breweries bearing the Trappist designation in existence, six of which reside within Belgian borders.[45] These are typically the most sought after and revered of Belgian beers.

Saison / Farmhouse Ale

Saisons are bright, earthy, fruity beers that are great for drinking year-round. They are often tart and refreshing with low levels of sweetness and modest bitterness. Some are spiced but even then the fruit and earthen yeast aspects still tend to dominate the senses. Saisons and farmhouse ales are great gateway styles to use to get into sour beers.

COLOR: Varies but typically Light Yellow ALCOHOL: Medium SWEETNESS: Low BITTERNESS: Medium HOPPINESS: Medium MALTINESS: Low FRUITINESS: Medium to High SPICINESS: Medium

Widely Available Examples: Ommegang Hennepin (Farmhouse Saison), Boulevard Brewing Tank 7 Farmhouse Ale, Goose Island Sofie

My Personal Picks: Hill Farmstead Florence, The Lost Abbey Red Barn Ale, Goose Island Pepe Nero, Goose Island Sofie, Kane Brewing Nom De Plume, Firestone Walker Opal – Proprietor's Reserve*, The Bruery Saison Rue

Belgian Pale Ale / Strong Pale Ale

Belgian Pale Ales tend to be both balanced and distinct in their flavors and aromas. Some are sweet, others are malty, and most are known for exhibiting aesthetically pleasing white heads when poured properly. A noticeable spice character often comes from the yeast and hops, balanced by the malt backbone. They are typically less bitter than American or English Pale Ales and have a crisp, refreshing finish. Strong Pale Ales tend to be dominated by a potent alcohol presence while still delivering the same aforementioned qualities as regular Belgian Pale Ales.

COLOR: Pale Yellow to Dark Gold ALCOHOL: Medium to High SWEETNESS: Low to Medium BITTERNESS: Medium HOPPINESS: Medium MALTINESS: Medium FRUITINESS: Medium SPICINESS: Medium

Widely Available Examples

(*Belgian Pale Ale*): Spencer Trappist Ale, Abbaye de Leffe S.A. Leffe Blonde, Brouwerij Palm NV Palm / Palm Speciale

(*Belgian Strong Pale Ale*): Brooklyn Brewery Local 1, Brasserie d'Achouffe La Chouffe, Goose Island Matilda

My Personal Picks:

(*Belgian Pale Ale*): Orval Trappist Ale, Russian River Redemption, Lost Abbey Saints' Devotion Ale, Ommegang Rare Vos (Amber Ale)

(*Belgian Strong Pale Ale*): Brouwerij Duvel Moortgat NV Duvel, Brouwerij Van Steenberge N.V. Piraat Ale, Brouwerij Huyghe Delirium Tremens, Unibroue Don De Dieu, Russian River Damnation

Belgian Dark Ale / Strong Dark Ale

The differences between Belgian Pale Ales and Dark Ales are considerable: whereas many new drinkers will find the pale ales to be easily accessible just as many will find the dark ales difficult to swallow. Yeast and spice tend to dominate the dark ales along with a bready malt quality. Alcohol can strangle the bouquet in stronger versions and can mask many of the other flavors found in less potent examples. Though potentially tough to get into, Belgian Dark Ales offer a great assortment of pleasant dark, pitted fruit notes.

COLOR: Light to Dark Brown ALCOHOL: Medium to High SWEETNESS: Low to Medium BITTERNESS: Low to Medium

HOPPINESS: Medium MALTINESS: Medium to High

FRUITINESS: Medium SPICINESS: Medium to High

Widely Available Examples

(*Belgian Dark Ale*): River Horse Belgian Freeze Belgian Style Winter Ale, Unibroue Noire De Chambly / Chambly Noire

(*Belgian Strong Dark Ale*): North Coast Brother Thelonious, Trappist Rochefort 8, Tröegs Mad Elf

My Personal Picks:

(*Belgian Dark Ale*): Ommegang Chocolate Indulgence Stout, Ithaca Cold Front

(*Belgian Strong Dark Ale*): Dogfish Head Raison d'Extra*, Dogfish Head Raison d'Etra, Brouwerij Het Anker Cuvée Van De Keizer Blauw (Blue), Chimay Grande Réserve (Blue), Unibroue Trois Pistoles, Maudite, or La Terrible, Brouwerij Van Steenberge N.V. Gulden Draak (Dark Triple), Brouwerij Huyghe Delirium Noël or Nocturnum, Allagash Black

Dubbel

Dubbel is a Trappist style of beer that began as a stronger version of a brown beer brewed by the Trappist Abbey of Westmalle in 1856.[46] It is closest in composition to the Belgian Strong Dark Ale but lacks the trademark dark fruitiness of the latter. Dubbels exhibit caramel-like sweetness bolstered by a full body and mouthfeel along with heavy maltiness. They are typically higher than average in alcohol content and carbonation.

COLOR: Dark Amber to Dark Brown ALCOHOL: Medium to High SWEETNESS: Medium BITTERNESS: Low to Medium HOPPINESS: Low MALTINESS: Medium to High FRUITINESS: Medium to High SPICINESS: Medium

Widely Available Examples: Ommegang (Abbey Ale), Westmalle Trappist Dubbel, Trappistes Rochefort 6, Allagash Dubbel Ale

My Personal Picks: Chimay Première (Red) Bières, Trappistes Rochefort 6, The Lost Abbey Lost & Found Abbey Ale

Tripel

Tripels are dangerously delicious golden ales that pack a serious alcohol wallop. They are fragrantly fruity on the nose and incredibly balanced between malts and hops. Fruity esters coalesce with sweetness from Belgian candi sugar and pale malts. The best tripels are deceptive in their potency masking their near double-digit abv in a complex mélange of intoxicating aromas and flavors. Tripels are among my favorite types of beer and are excellent for sipping slowly!

COLOR: Vibrant Yellow to Golden ALCOHOL: High SWEETNESS: Medium BITTERNESS: Medium HOPPINESS: Medium MALTINESS: Low FRUITINESS: Medium to High SPICINESS: Low

Widely Available Examples: Westmalle Trappist Tripel, Victory Golden Monkey, Chimay Tripel (White), St. Bernardus Tripel, Brouwerij Het Anker Gouden Carolus Tripel

My Personal Picks: Tripel Karmeliet, Unibroue La Fin Du Monde, Westmalle Trappist Tripel, Maredsous 10 – Tripel, Allagash Curieux (Bourbon Barrel-Aged Tripel)

Quadrupel

Quadrupels (or Quads) are among my top five favorite styles of beer. They are typically the strongest Belgian style beer made, combining the dark fruitiness of the vaunted dubbel with the alcoholic vigor of tripels. Garnet or dark reddish brown in color, they are alluring in their appearances and their aromas, which are redolent with dark fruit and unabashed alcohol punch. They are as sweet as dubbels or Belgian strong dark ales but, in my opinion, are *far* smoother even with their double-digit abv. Few beers are as sippable by fireside on a cold winter's night as a noxious quadruple!

COLOR: Deep Amber or Garnet to Dusky Brown

ALCOHOL: High SWEETNESS: Medium to High BITTERNESS: Low HOPPINESS: Low MALTINESS: Medium to High FRUITINESS: Medium to High SPICINESS: Low

Widely Available Examples: St. Bernardus Abt 12, Trappistes Rochefort 10, Ommegang Three Philosophers Belgian Style Blend (Quadrupel), Boulevard Brewing The Sixth Glass

My Personal Picks: The Lost Abbey Judgment Day, Trappistes Rochefort 10, Kane Brewing Quad

(BONUS: Trappist Westvleteren 12 (XII)* (*notoriously difficult to come by!*), Firestone Walker Stickee Monkee* (*bourbon barrel aged*), Weyerbacher Blasphemy (*whiskey barrel aged*), Kane Brewing Anniversary Beer* (*various spirits*), Boulevard Brewing Bourbon Barrel Quad (BBQ) (*bourbon barrel aged*))

SOUR BEERS

Sour beers offer a truly unique drinking experience for the craft beer explorer. Many of these are fermented wildly while others are imbued with very specific strains of bacteria to produce mouth-puckering, eye-watering tart sourness. Some are aged on fruit to provide a balancing degree of sweetness while others stand completely on their own in unapologetic, shameless sour glory. True sours are wood-barrel aged and are thus imbued with an earthy sweetness. Arguably the *most* acquired of acquired tastes, sours offer equal rewards for the effort put into demystifying their complexities.

There are a multitude of sour beer styles with a huge amount of differentiation from one example to the next, which neuters the efficacy of a list of suggestions. American Wild Ales, Lambics, Goses, and Berliner Weissbiers are among the most common however so if you happen to see one of these on a beer menu and you are feeling adventurous then be sure to give it a shot! Many who have embarked upon the strange journey into sour beers have found themselves transformed into insatiable fanatics, myself included!

A far more comprehensive list of styles is available online at http://www.beeradvocate.com/beer/style/ as a part of

BeerAdvocate's educative beer section. There, you will find brief

informative blurbs about each style along with an exhaustive list of

examples. As of this writing there are 104 styles listed though I have

tried 111 different styles overall!

At first blush, it may seem like the act of tasting beer is a three step process: open mouth, pour in beer, and swallow. When you're dealing with relatively flavorless, watered down, mass produced brews then that is undoubtedly an appropriate approach; when you are dealing with a beer that is painstakingly *crafted*, however, with immense attention to detail and high quality ingredients, then a more nuanced, comprehensive approach is warranted. Taking the time to taste a beer properly not only maximizes your drinking experience and the possible pleasure derived from it but it also helps you to learn more about beer in general; understanding why certain things are the way that they are and picking up on commonalities between beers will ultimately help you to develop your palate faster and more completely than blindly swigging out of a pint glass or bottle.

Using the Proper Glassware

Pairing the proper vessel with the right beer is a critical component of beer tasting; the task can seem downright herculean though given the plethora of glassware options and equally multitudinous types of beers. Some glasses bolster the beer's bouquet, trapping it and releasing it as you sip. Others accentuate the appearance allowing for better head retention or residual lacing on the glass. Others still bear historical significance and are inextricably linked to a given beer, place, and time.

For our purposes here, I would recommend a simple **tulip glass** since it serves as a sort of all-purpose receptacle for nearly every type of beer. My go-to glass is the Samuel Adams Perfect Pint Glass since I've accrued a few from my visits to the brewery and so I would recommend that one but really any tulip glass should suffice. The benefit of the tulip over others is that the bowl at the top captures the beer's aroma and the shape (at least in my experience) and it helps in head retention (though it really does depend upon the individual beer). Supposedly the etching at the bottom of the glass helps to generate bubbles but I've never been able to tell whether it was the glass generating them or the beer's inherent carbonation. Regardless, it covers enough ground that you will get plenty of use out of it.

Read the Label

Craft beer labels are often at once entertaining and informative. Some breweries go to great lengths to put forth a memorable beer label or can design embodying the belief that attention to detail towards what goes on the *outside* belies an equal appreciation for the detail of what goes *inside* of it. Whether or not this is true is debatable because I've had some truly *awful* beer out of bottles and cans with truly gorgeous appearances and some unbelievably delicious beers out of some utterly forgettable ones. Still, I definitely appreciate the spirit of the sentiment even if some breweries place *too* much effort into and emphasis on their labels so as to detract from a subpar brew lurking within.

With that said some craft beer bottles and cans offer a wealth of information that can help you to paint a mental picture of the beer before you even pop the top. Some are facts and figures that would appeal mostly to the craft beer devotee but some are pertinent, necessary points that will shape your understanding of and appreciation for what you're about to drink. Among these bits of datum are the aforementioned abv, IBU, and SRM numbers along with the occasional OG (original gravity), FG (final gravity), and Degrees Plato. This latter trio pertains to the beer's density, which will essentially give you an idea of how alcoholic the beer is.

Other information might include the bottling date, a drink before or drink after date, the ideal serving temperature for the beer, and information regarding cellaring. Freshness is absolutely critical for certain styles (particularly well-hopped beers) with a huge discernible difference existing between an IPA that was bottled a few weeks ago versus a few months (the hops tend to fade and the malt comes more into focus the longer a hoppy beer sits in a can or bottle). Most beers will taste better if consumed before a certain date but a few breweries have begun posting drink *after* dates. Personally, I find this to be nothing more than a marketing gimmick and my attitude is that, if a brewer wanted you to drink the beer *after* a certain date then he or she should have conditioned it longer and released it to be available at that time.

Proper beer temperature is something that we will delve into a little further on but this too can have a huge impact on the beer's flavor and aroma. Cellaring is a topic that we will cover towards the end of this half of the book but, in a nutshell, it equates to aging a beer in the proper environment purposely for future consumption. Other than all of that, some breweries like Oskar Blues and The Other Half enjoy providing hidden messages for their consumers on the bottom of cans so be sure to sneak a peek the next time you pick one up!

The Perfect Pour

Pouring a beer properly out of a bottle or can has a great impact on both how quickly you can enjoy the fully actualized beer and how well you can detect the nuances. Pouring a beer too quickly or too vigorously will likely not only generate an overflow of fluffy head that will take time to settle back down, it can also affect the aromatics: too violent a pour can cause some of the more delicate but ultimately pleasing aspects of the beer to become muddied or lost. Pouring a beer too slowly can result in a flat, lusterless head that fails to produce the full mouthfeel that the beer was intended to offer and to spring those nuanced aromatics into action.

Now, some folks might ask why beer needs to be poured at all; these represent the straight from the bottle or can crowd. The primary reason for me is that so much is lost in the aroma which, as you'll see, is the second most important aspect of tasting beer. Secondarily, you lose out on the beer's aesthetics, which might or might not impact your enjoyment of the beer. With the exception of nitrogen-infused bottles like Guinness Draught and some of the newer shaped cans that allow for better aroma release, beers are better off being poured into a glass.

Technique-wise, the pour is simple: begin by holding a clean glass at a forty-five degree angle and tilt the bottle or can until it is almost horizontal and the beer begins to flow smoothly and steadily. Try to aim for the wall of the glass (typically halfway down) rather than the bottom and allow the beer to pour in at this angle until it reaches the midway point of the glass. Then, gradually straighten up the glass while continuing the same steady pour until there is roughly an inch or two of space (two fingers' worth) at the top. At this point, take a look at how much head has been created and adjust the speed of your pour accordingly: too little and you can speed it up, pouring directly into the center of the glass—too much and you can slow it down, even waiting for some of the head to dissipate before finishing. Ideally, you want between a half-inch and one inch of luscious, creamy foam sitting atop the beer.

Tasting With Your Eyes

Technically speaking, the first part of a proper beer tasting begins with the visual. A beer's optics gets you ready to taste the beer, giving you an idea based solely on its appearance of what you're going to enjoy. Typically, a darker beer is going to be maltier or even more roasted than a lighter one and so seeing such a beer will spring the requisite taste buds into gear. As we've noted already though a beer's color gives you only the most perfunctory of ideas of what it's going to taste like (three identically golden yellow beers can have three very different tastes and aromas despite their indiscernible appearances).

Personally, I find the visual element to be the least important at least when I am trying new beers. If I'm craving a rich, dark, super malty stout and I pour one into my glass, I *will* get excited by the beer's appearance but that's because I already know what to expect. I've had enough experiences with misleading beers to know that my *nose* is the organ that will tell me the most about the beer pre-sip. (*Carton Brewing's Regular Coffee for example looks like an IPA but smells like a glass of iced coffee as does Stone Brewing's Master of Disguise Imperial Golden Stout. Firestone Walker's Wookey Jack by contrast looks like a roasty porter but is an absolute hop burst of a black ale. Looks can be deceiving!*)

Using Your Nose

Nothing gets me more excited about tasting a beer than the first intoxicating whiff. I know that might sound counterintuitive but in my experience the best beers have tremendous bouquets that segue into even better tastes; conversely, some of the worst beers that I've ever had alerted me to that fact before they even touched my tongue. A beer's aroma will tell you a lot about what is to come whether it's how hoppy it might be, how sweet or fruity, and even how roasted and malty. The sweet caramel and vanilla notes in certain darker beers for example are both evident and redolent in the *nose*, which will bring the sweetness-activated taste buds to full attention.

In order to cull the most out of your first few inhalations, it is imperative that the beer be agitated first. A few gentle swirls should be enough to release the aromatics which, if the proper glassware was used, will become trapped towards the top. I generally raise the glass to my nose close enough so that I can detect the beer's various aromas without allowing my nose to dip inside (though this has happened before much to my chagrin). A single deep breath with a gentle exhalation should be enough to allow you to get an idea of what the beer will be offering. Subsequent sniffs can be shorter and less spaced out but two or three generally work for me. It's important to take at least two because your brain has to process a lot of sensory information during the first one and so you might miss some of the intricacies that future breaths will offer.

Though you might not have thought of it, your nose is arguably the most important factor in taste and how you perceive it aside from your actual taste buds. Think about the last time you had a cold or nasal congestion—you likely were incapable of tasting whatever it was that you were eating to the same degree that you would have in better health. Plus, for people of my generation and older, there was the dreaded taste of medicine as children. How did we avoid tasting it? We pinched our noses and held our breath when we drank it, exhaling only after we swallowed our chaser of water or juice to mask the medicinal flavor!

What I love most about exploring a beer's bouquet though is the sort of hypothesis that it creates in my mind before the taste. A beer that is dry hopped extremely well might be remarkably fragrant in its hop floralness but then the actual taste could feature a fruitier or more resinous flavor. Subsequent sniffs and sips allow me to figure out just what is going on the beer and to determine whether some of the aromas are in sync with the flavors that might be causing them or if they exist as esoteric entities unto themselves. I'll then ponder how the brewers managed to elicit those particular qualities in one aspect but not the other. Either way, you do not have to be a beer nerd to appreciate a beer's aroma and its importance in the overall drinking experience!

The First Sip

Dilated pupils; sweaty palms; rapid breathing: these are the tell-tale signs of many of our firsts. It could be prom night, a job interview, or, in our case here, the excitement of a first sip of a legendary beer. To get the most out of this auspicious occasion though it pays to understand how our mouths work and the different duties our taste buds collectively undertake. It drives me nuts when I see people taking teensy-tiny, peckish little sips through pursed, pensive lips just as much as the big gulpers; there's a certain merit to restraint and proper tasting technique just as there is for pouring and choosing the right glass.

In the case of tasting a beer, you want to take a big enough sip so that the liquid can reach all of the parts of your mouth but not too large so that it fills the cavity. You also want to open your lips wide enough to allow some air to enter as you sip as this will help to trap some of the aromas inside thus accentuating the flavor. Swirling the beer inside of your mouth before you swallow is important because it ensures that all of the necessary taste buds will come into contact with the beer.

The sensation of the beer is almost as important as its taste; this is where your cheeks come into play. A beer's mouthfeel is a critical quality to consider in terms of how much you will enjoy drinking it: some beers have a very full, creamy mouthfeel while others are thinner or waterier. Certain mouthfeels benefit certain styles better than others: I like my sips of Russian imperial stouts to feel massive and full whereas I prefer my witbiers on the thinner side. Therefore, when I encounter a really thin-feeling stout or an overly heavy witbier, I do not derive as much enjoyment out of the beer as I would have otherwise.

Obviously the single most important aspect of any beer is how it tastes; this is where the taste buds come into play. The popular belief is that the tongue is divided into quadrants or zones where certain aspects are detected at different points. I can neither confirm nor deny the veracity of this but science does not seem to support the claim. With that said, regardless of *where* you encounter them, the major flavors that the tongue detects are sweet, sour, bitter, salty, and umami. Coat the entire tongue and you're guaranteeing yourself that you'll be able to pick up on all of the various flavors in a given beer.

Temperature

A beer's taste changes with its temperature: the colder the beer, the more its details are masked—the warmer it is, to a degree (ha!), the more vivacious and varied the nuances. As a general rule, you want your beer cold but not *too* cold. Certain beer styles benefit from higher serving temperatures while others tend to degrade as they warm. Though there is no firm rule-of-thumb to follow when it comes to beers and their temperatures, I feel like higher alcohol beers benefit more from warming while lower ones do not, regardless of style. For example, I prefer my hoppy beers to go straight from the refrigerator into my glass but I'll slow-play my imperial IPAs to give them some breathing room and to allow the alcohol to shine through a little more.

With other alcoholically robust styles like barleywines and imperial stouts, the actual *flavors* can alter greatly with warmth;

barrel aged beers, in particular, benefit the most from a gradual rise in temperature. Certain aspects such as the vanilla and oaky notes of a bourbon barrel aged beer will become enhanced as they warm; the dark fruity aspects of barleywines tend to become more prominent as the alcoholic notes slowly mellow out near room temperature. There is undeniably an element of trial-and-error when it comes to serving temperature but if you're going to have a beer that might sit for a while then I would recommend going for one that is higher in abv.

Recently, more attention has been paid to glassware's impact on temperature changes. Teku glasses have grown exponentially in popularity both because of their aesthetic appeal and their functionality; the glass stem allows a drinker to hold the glass without affecting the temperature of the beer inside of it. By holding a traditional glass (tulips included), you're transferring your body heat from your hand into the glass and thus into the beer. Personally, I don't obsess over temperature to that extent and I generally drink beers that grow more complex as they warm and are typically higher in alcohol so I'm drinking them slowly anyway so this is less of a concern to me than for others but it's a point worth noting nonetheless.

Ultimately there are a slew of factors that affect a beer's flavor and the experience of tasting it. Some are beyond our control as drinkers but many are influenced directly by our actions whether it is the way we pour, the type of glass that we use, or what temperature we serve the beer at. Taking care to consider these aspects will help to ensure that you get the most out of the beer that you put your hard-earned money into enjoying!

HOW TO GET THE MOST OUT OF CRAFT BEER

Craft beer has become one of my most ardent passions because it is an easy hobby to get into and offers a nearly inexhaustible amount of variety; there is always something fun to do or an interesting way of engaging with beer. As with any hobby, there are different degrees of interest and ability: for every Cicerone certified beer connoisseur there is a fresh face walking into a craft brewery for the very first time. Some folks fall in love with a particular beer or style and will stick *only* to that while others like myself are constantly finding new favorites. You can be a ticker (someone who seeks to cover as much ground as possible, valuing the number of beers sampled versus a deeper understanding of the beers themselves) or a whale hunter (someone who seeks out extremely rare beers both for the thrill of it and the rewards reaped).

Regardless of your level of interest, there is something fun that you can do to enhance your enjoyment of craft beer. Once you've gotten your feet wet, you might feel comfortable exploring things a little more deeply. Here are some suggestions to help you to get the most out of your adventures:

HOST YOUR OWN TASTING

Inviting others over to share in your hobby is a great way to enjoy it and to further your own beer education. It can be as simple as visiting your local bottle shop or liquor store and picking blindly off of the shelves or it can be far more in-depth. You can select a single brewery and sample a variety of their offerings or you can go with a particular style and find multiple examples to taste side-by-side. With a little planning, you can do what's called a **vertical tasting** where you try multiple *vintages* of the same beer simultaneously; this is fun especially after you've built up some experience because you can appreciate the subtleties that separate one year from the next.

Hosting your own tasting event serves not only to expose your friends to craft beer but it also invites you to think more critically about the beer you're exploring. Jotting down tasting notes for comparison purposes and for future reference gives more value to the experience and encourages deeper conversation about the beers. You can keep track of the label information (abv, IBU, SRM, etc.) but more importantly you can take notes about the actual tasting experience. Just follow the steps from the How To Taste Beer section in this book and write down your reaction to each one!

WRITE ABOUT BEER

If you enjoy writing then you can put the information from your tastings to good use by writing up individual beer reviews on websites like BeerAdvocate or Rate Beer or by maintaining your own blog. When I started my blog "The Beer Whisperers" (http://www.thebeerwhisperers.com) I found that I started to pay more attention to the minutiae of my drinking experiences and felt encouraged to attend more beer events with the intention of writing reviews for others to enjoy.

Once again, such an act invites interaction and conversation about the beer and it provides others with alternative perspectives to reflect upon. Plus, it's fun to wax nostalgic and to look back upon the beers you reviewed early on and to see whether or not your opinion about them has changed with time and experience.

KEEP A BEER LIST

I've always been a sucker for lists. Whether it's a top ten list or something more comprehensive, I derive a lot of enjoyment from exploring lists pertaining to things that I like. I suppose that it goes hand-in-hand with my collector's mentality and perfectionism—that there is some sense of accomplishment to be found in completing a set of something. As such, when I realized nearly ten years ago that I was beginning to accrue a number of different beers, I started a database to keep track of them all; more than 3,500 beers later, I'm glad that I did!

Keeping a beer list allows you not just an opportunity for reflection but also a practical resource for understanding your likes and dislikes. For *my* list, I maintain the requisite information about the beer like its name, the brewery that makes it, and where it's from but more importantly I also give it a grade and keep a notes field to record my reaction. Since I'm always on the lookout for trying new beers it also helps me to avoid repeating brews that I might not want to try again.

USE BEER APPS ON YOUR PHONE

There are a number of great craft beer-related apps available but by far the best is Untappd. It's a great way to keep a list of beers that you've tried with a user-friendly interface that is a perfect fit for our modern social media-centric society. Check in a beer, give it a grade, toast others on *their* check-ins, and unlock badges for different styles and a multitude of other beer-related miscellany. It's an excellent way to keep tabs on your beers and to interact with other craft beer friends throughout the country.

JOIN AN ONLINE BEER COMMUNITY

BeerAdvocate is the premiere resource for all-things-beer and it also features a lively, active user-base that engages daily on the forums. It's an excellent place to learn about beer, to discuss it, and just to find likeminded individuals who share your passion. I rely solely on BeerAdvocate's database of beers as a reference point for my own data and recommend checking them out along with their awesome eponymous print magazine.

Facebook too features a variety of beer themed groups and Instagram is a great place to follow your fellow craft fanatics.

EXPLORE YOUR LOCAL BEER SCENE

According to the Brewers Association, "75% of adults live within 10 miles of a craft brewery."[47] I myself live within a half an hour of more than a dozen breweries in a state that is still at the tail end of the craft beer movement. Almost regardless of where you live you'll be able to find a brewery to check out. Supporting your local brewery is great for both the craft beer community and the one at large because you're helping to sustain a small business and you're encouraging growth at a time when the biggest macrobreweries are trying gradually to dominate the market by buying out the small guys.

Drinking at the brewery itself gives you the opportunity to consume the absolute freshest beer you're likely to encounter. Most places that allow for on-site consumption will offer a variety of pour sizes so you can either knock back some pints with your friends or slow play a sampler or two. Many breweries also allow for take-away beer in the form of growlers, bottles, or cans, which means you that you can partake in that same ultra-fresh beer at home.

FIND A GREAT CRAFT BEER BAR OR RESTAURANT

If drinking at a brewery doesn't jive with you then you can always consider seeking out a dedicated craft beer bar or a craft beer-focused restaurant. My wife and I fell in love with Cloverleaf Tavern in Caldwell, New Jersey after a friend referred us to their "M.B.A. (Master of Beer Appreciation)" program. Though we lived in New York at the time, we loved the place and the people there so much that we made it our favorite and most frequented spot when the craft beer mood struck us (despite the ninety minute round trip drive!)

Many such locations offer programs like mug clubs where, for a nominal fee, you can have your own personal beer vessel on site, often with other perks like discounted or larger pours or beer appreciation programs. For us, the M.B.A. program perfectly suited our passion at the time. When we each completed the forty-five beer syllabus, our names were added to the plaques on the wall and we embarked upon our Ph.Ds (Professor of Hops and Draughts). Though the perks and freebies that came with the program are undeniably awesome, it was the experience of trying all of those beers and discussing them with the knowledgeable servers and staff at the restaurant that made it worthwhile.

TAKE A BEER ROAD TRIP

The best way to explore craft beer is to take an expedition to as many breweries as you can. There is so much to be absorbed from visiting places, particularly out-of-state ones, because you can learn about the local drinking (and other) culture while checking out beer from new regions. We've undertaken several "Beer & Baseball" summer road trips where we visited new Major League Baseball stadiums and a slew of breweries along the way. Having a designated driver and limiting consumption are obvious necessities for such an adventure so be sure to plan accordingly!

ATTEND A BEER FESTIVAL

Some of the most fun I've ever had as a craft beer fan came at events hosted by Dogfish Head at their Milton, Delaware brewery. Sam Calagione and company know how to throw a party and I look back fondly on those occasions as much for the great local food and music I got to enjoy as I do the beer itself. Larger events like the Great American Beer Fest in Denver and the Extreme Beer Fest in Boston afford attendees the opportunity to try festival-only beers and quite often the chance to sample rarities that others only dream of trying (Founders' CBS and Sam Adams' Utopias to name but two!)

EXPERIMENT WITH BEER BLENDS

Blending beer is an age-old practice but it can be fun to do with a modern twist and equipment. You can make your own Black & Tans either with a spoon or one of the numerous contraptions available; the trick is to fill the pint glass halfway with the heavier beer (typically Bass Ale) and then to pour the less viscous beer (in this case, Guinness Draught) slowly over the back of the spoon held over the pint glass. Another popular and less complicated blend is to take Young's Double Chocolate Stout (purple label) and to blend it with Well's Banana Bread Beer (yellow label); this combination has become popular enough that the two beers are often found situated together on the shelf.

My favorite alteration variation is to use Dogfish Head's Randall Jr. to infuse beers with other ingredients. The strainer allows you to imbue a single serving of beer with whatever flavors you would like without sullying the beer itself when it goes into your glass. You can transform that humdrum Russian Imperial Stout by letting it sit on some Madagascar bourbon vanilla beans or infuse that pedestrian porter with some delicious Sumatran coffee. If heat is more your thing then throw some jalapeños or habaneros in there and spice things up!

COOK WITH BEER

Some beers are worthy of having entire meals developed around them while others are perfectly suited for serving as ingredients in dishes of your own design. Beer can be used in place of other liquids or in addition to with certain styles providing more to some dishes than others (Guinness Draught, for example, is simply divine for use in beef stew or shepherd's pie!) Learning about how to draw the right flavors and elements out of your beer can be a fun way of improving your culinary skills while expanding your craft beer knowledge. My "Beer Can Chicken" has certainly been a hit with my friends and family thanks to Maui Brewing's CoCoNut Porter!

BREW YOUR OWN BEER

Mainstream home brewing has come a long way from the days of gag gift brewing setups. Home brewing is a fun, easy, and exciting way to learn more about beer. Can't find a particular style that really does it for you? Then just make your own! For under a hundred dollars you can put together a suitable setup that you can use in your kitchen to make whatever your heart desires.

If you're interested in dipping your feet in the home brewing pool then I would recommend seeking out a local home brewing supply store. The people there are likely as passionate about brewing as they are knowledgeable and will prove to be an invaluable resource both in terms of physical materials and intangible support. I wouldn't have had nearly as much fun or success with my own home brewing ventures were it not for Ron and his crew at Love2Brew in North Brunswick, New Jersey!

There is an overwhelming amount of helpful information available online and in book form but by far the most useful book for the novice home brewer is "How To Brew" by John Palmer. If you're even *remotely* interested in home brewing then this is the must-buy resource for you. As a bonus suggestion, I'd recommend Sam Calagione's Extreme Brewing because of the invaluable and illustrious color photographs that accompany a slew of recipes including some for actual Dogfish Head beers like 60 Minute IPA and Midas Touch. Plus, the focus is on liquid malt extract-based home brewing rather than all-grain, which is what most people typically start out with (and requires a less expensive, simpler assortment of equipment!)

Regardless of how you interact with craft beer, just make sure you enjoy it! Sláinte!

Disclaimer: I'm not a fitness expert nor do I have any formal training. I have no affiliation with any company or product. Instead, I'm someone who has accrued a ton of experience in the gym and in life through trial and error. The programs, products, and methodologies that I promote come from my personal experience with and affinity for these things because I have found them to be useful in my own journey. They are all merely suggestions to be considered and not rules to be followed absolutely. My goal is to get you started on your own path and so I am offering insight into the things that ultimately got me started on mine and that keep me moving ever forward along it.

As with any changes to your diet or activity level, please consult with your doctor or an expert in the requisite field before engaging in any new, drastic alterations to your lifestyle. Listen to your body and react accordingly if you do not feel comfortable with whatever adjustments you make to your eating or exercising habits. The goal is to make positive, long-term, long-lasting changes and to minimize both discomfort and personal endangerment.

FITNESS

Modern America has become a veritable Garden of Eden—rife with plenty of things to make our lives easier and more enjoyable but also laden with temptation. We wander aimlessly about with our faces buried in our smart phones, desperately lost amid virtual worlds of our own design. People are paying ever more attention to their newsfeeds and social media followers while focusing less on their own general well-being, especially when it comes to their levels of fitness and eating habits.

It has become almost impossible to avoid the temptations of unhealthy food. Walk around any major city or drive along the Interstate and you're sure to come across a restaurant offering cheap, delicious, fat-laden, calorie rich grub. These places offer us convenience and feel-good food that we just can't seem to get enough of; simply put, we don't know when to stop or how to say no to the things that are bad for us.

The same can be said about things like sugar-soaked soda and the seemingly endless array of snack foods that are at our disposal often at a nominal expense. These items are grouped together at the supermarket dominating entire aisles while healthier options are relegated to a few shelves often completely at the other end of the store. These foods and beverages are sold at a premium and are marketed as boutique items that convey more about social status than dietary decisions; healthy living has become synonymous with some new age, hipster-oriented way of life that necessitates expensive food overrun with qualifiers like organic, fair-trade, free-range, cage-free, vegan, and countless others.

As the collective American waistband has expanded so have our individual levels of self-esteem shrunk. We are creatures of habit who wish desperately to make changes that appear easy for others to enact but which seem impossible for ourselves to execute. We are told to live healthier lifestyles but have not been given the tools necessary to make such an adjustment nor the road map for how to do so.

Plenty of attention has been paid to *what* we eat and drink but not necessarily to *how* we enjoy these things. Obviously there are some things that are better for us and some that are worse but our level of health is determined more by the degree to which we consume these things and in what proportion. Many people opt for so-called low calorie or lite foods without realizing that they often replace fat with sugar or something else to improve the taste. They then over-consume thinking that, because they are eating something that is purportedly *better* for them, that they can then eat more of it; it is this mindset that has led to an epidemic of poor eating habits and their enormous consequences.

Somewhere along the line, slimming down has become an unnecessarily complex, esoteric activity—one that stymies the majority of Americans based upon recent obesity rates; the problem isn't limited to adults either. According to the CDC, one in every five children between the ages of 6 and 19 is considered obese.[48] Since the 1970s, obesity rates among children ages 2-5 and 12-19 have tripled while rates for 6-11 year old children have nearly *quintupled*.[49] There are a number of factors at the heart of the issue but it is fair to say that modeling the behavior of the adults in their lives is certainly among them: in 2013-2014, **70.7%** of American adults 20 and older were considered overweight with more than half of them being deemed obese.[50]

I believe that weight-gain related problems in this country stem as much from habit as from anything else; people over-consume with regularity while failing to extend any effort towards balancing out that excess through exercise. They expend ever more time seeking enjoyment from tacit sources of entertainment tuning *in* to their digital lives as a way of tuning *out* the stressors in their actual ones. They feel bad about how they look and how they feel and so they seek solace in things that will make them feel better; all too often though those things are high calorie foods and drink as well as passive entertainment. I know because I counted myself among them for more than a decade.

Making a change to a healthier lifestyle can be one of if not the single most difficult thing we can do in modern America. We see others succeed and so we are encouraged to try and yet we fail miserably falling back into the same unhealthy ruts that we've buried ourselves in. There is no shortage of feel-good motivation and well-intended advice floating around about how to make those changes—things that many would consider to be so-called commonsense. If that were the case though and if it really was that simple then wouldn't we *all* be that much healthier?

The reality is that our habits die hard—particularly those that bring us pleasure. A soda with dinner or a six pack on the weekend might seem like they help us get through our days but I assure you that it is simply a matter of perspective; we allow ourselves to be deceived by our own predilections for things that taste good and thus make us seemingly *feel* good. I know because it's a lie that I told myself repeatedly as I justified eating and drinking decisions that I knew weren't just bad but were ultimately harmful for my body and my psyche.

Everyone wants to lose weight but few of us seem to achieve the personal transformations we desire; fewer still seem capable of committing to those changes for the long term. We've lived through countless fad diets and workout crazes and yet here we are still loosening our belts. There might never be a single catchall solution that will lead everyone to healthier and consequently happier lives but after *years* of struggling I believe that I have found *mine*.

The purpose of this section of the book is not to provide some providential panacea to help you to lose weight or to enact positive change in your life because there *isn't one*. There is no magic program or product that will do the work for you. Instead, my goal here is to offer a roadmap to your own personal metamorphoses by offering up what I have learned through my successes and my failures. While my particular mode of transformation might not work for *you*, it might still serve as a catalyst for your own journey or at the very least give you a different point-of-view that might positively influence your own.

MY WEIGHT LOSS STORY

When I was a teenager, basketball was my life. Throughout high school, I played an average of forty hours a week during the school year and even more during breaks. Aside from that, I worked out almost daily, routinely embarked upon long bike rides, and had a generally high level of fitness; once I started college though everything changed.

I began my freshman year at Baruch College weighing between 150 and 160 lbs at a height of 6 feet tall; I graduated four years later nearly forty pounds heavier. Part of the adjustment in my size and shape stemmed from an abrupt change in lifestyle. Commuting from southern Brooklyn into Manhattan every day left me with a dearth of free time that I had previously used for exercise. I was also suddenly surrounded by a plethora of delicious but unhealthy food options; my once healthy habits were devolving into lazy gluttony.

My rising stress levels and responsibilities coupled with an ever-ebbing supply of willpower resulting in a slew of poor eating decisions and excuses. I was dealing with a lot in my personal life at the time and I knew that something had to give; unfortunately, that something was working out. I spent less time being active and more time in the pursuit of artificial gratification in the form of food and drink.

In my early twenties, I drank a fair amount but rarely to excess. I've always chosen my booze based upon how it tastes rather than its potency or alcoholic effect. I thus favored sweet mixed drinks and consequently piled on even more pounds through the calorie-rich, sugar-laden swill I swallowed with reckless abandon.

Fast-forward to 2013 and my personal nadir. Throughout the previous dozen years, I would go through spurts of activity when my spirits were low. I would work out for a bit but managed always to set myself up for failure. I still had the mentality of that fit teenager that I once was but not the physique to match it. I would push myself too hard without engaging in the proper preparation or utilizing any sort of recovery and ultimately I would either get injured or would burn out.

I was growing tired of the ebb and flow of self-esteem—of the seemingly insurmountable battle with myself over what I ate and drank. I would give up some of the obvious culprits that were causing my weight-gain—whether it was whiskey or soda, junk food or takeout. Inevitably though I would go back to whatever it was I eschewed sometimes with even *more* fervor than before.

Healthy eating and drinking seemed to enjoy an inverse relationship with my stress level: as the latter would rise, the former would diminish. In the back of my mind I *knew* that I was hurting myself and yet I felt like I was incapable of doing anything about it. The serotonin bumps that I would get from a doughnut at breakfast or a few drinks over the weekend propelled me through some taxing times and so I decided to ignore the signals my mind and body were sending me.

By the end of 2012, I had hit 230 lbs—my all-time highest weight. A year and a half earlier, I had lost some significant girth by going through Beachbody's P90X program with a friend. To my utter dismay though I had gained back all of the weight by the end of the year; only a few weeks into 2013, I had finally had enough.

On February 6th, 2013, I began my journey to a happier, healthier, more confident me. It was an overcast day with the temperature just above freezing as I stepped out for my first Couch-to-5K workout. I had heard great things about the program from people who had tried it and more importantly I saw the results. I enjoyed doing P90X but I knew that the time commitment was too great for me to expect reasonably that I would be able to complete it a second time; it was the first dose of much needed honesty with myself.

The C25K program required a mere thirty minutes and change per workout three times a week for a little more than two months—something that I had absolutely no excuse for failing to complete. I was dubious of the achingly gradual progress that the workouts employed but at the same time I thought that I might benefit from such a deliberate pace; after all, every time I had tried to work out in the past I immediately put the pedal to the floor each time to my detriment. And so I set out on day one.

Every workout begins with a brisk five-minute warm up walk. I threw myself into the first one with equal parts enthusiasm and effort. I felt good, both physically because I was finally active again but also emotionally; something seemed different this time. My high spirits carried me to the end of that initial stroll when the chime rang out and a pleasant feminine voice told me to begin running.

The first three workouts consisted of sixty seconds of jogging followed by ninety seconds of walking. This sounded a bit too easy but I had promised myself that I would not only stick to the program but follow every directive exactly as instructed. I figured that the worst case scenario was that I would breeze through the first few workouts and be primed for the more difficult stuff later on. After all, it was *one minute* of running—how hard could it be?

Fifty seconds into that first sixty second run I thought I was going to die. I could hardly breathe and my mouth was as arid as an Arizona desert. The voice of self-recrimination in my mind was vociferous and vicious in its dressing down of my pitiful state. Deep down, I knew that this was the worst shape I had ever been in. I knew how pathetic it was that I could hardly last a single minute of running but—**and this is a seminal moment in my transformation**—I embraced that negativity and owned it. *I* had gotten myself here and I was the ***sole*** reason that that run was so difficult.

I dug deep into my mental and physical reserves and gutted out the final ten seconds refusing to fail on my very first run; it was a moment of precedence that would prove invaluable over the next

140

three years. As soon as the chime sounded, I began walking, stunned by my physical state; I had always hated running but this was a new low. I did my best to catch my breath before the suddenly all-too-short ninety second walk was done and I was back to running.

Ultimately, I made it through that first workout humbled but hopeful. Fatigued as I was, I felt like I had finally stumbled upon the right path for myself. I made it through each workout and improved more rapidly than I had anticipated. I encountered setbacks along the way—runs that I was unable to complete on my first attempt but that which I ultimately tackled the next time around. Then, ten weeks after I started, I successfully completed my graduation 5K run.

I was utterly elated and proud of myself for the first time. I wasted no time in downloading the Couch-to-10K program and continued my workouts having finally fallen in love with running—an act that I had abhorred seemingly forever. I had accomplished what I had set out to do and I felt unstoppable.

And so it was that on Memorial Day weekend in 2013 I flew fleet-footed through the forest along a primitive trail in Hartshorne Woods after a day of hiking. I had wanted to undertake a challenging black diamond trail and found one at the park. I ignored the warnings that it was designed for hikers and not runners and set out for what I expected to be a quick jog through the woods; it was a fateful decision to say the least.

Somewhere along the way, my foot came down upon a rock that lay hidden beneath leaves and dirt. As my ankle buckled, I heard what sounded like a shotgun blast followed by an equally loud scream; I was shocked to realize a moment later that it was me who had uttered such a shriek. I pulled up from my run crying out in shock and denial, gripping my ankle as tightly as I wanted to strangle myself at that moment for my stupidity. As an avid hiker, the one piece of advice I had always heeded and always proffered was never to go hiking alone. Worse, I had decided to leave my phone in the car since it was going to be a "quick" jog. Suddenly, I found myself in the middle of the woods on a stone-strewn path far from help with no way of communicating with my family who were waiting for me back in the parking lot.

I sat down on a boulder, collected myself, and assessed the situation. My ankle was already beginning to swell so I undid the laces on my sneaker and retied it as tightly as I could knowing that it was imperative that I maintain pressure. I had two choices: I could try to crawl up through the bramble along the steep slope that led back to a paved path or I could go back the way that I came. I decided to try the more difficult ascent and managed to get close enough to the road to hear the voices of pedestrians passing above me. It didn't take long for the voices to recede and silence to return though and I realized that it would be foolish to try to climb any higher; to do so would not only endanger myself but anyone who might try to help me out. I had gotten myself into this mess and I refused to drag anyone else down into it with me.

Sliding back down to the trail, I tightened my other sneaker and began a steady hobble-hop back the way that I had come. I wasn't sure how far I had made it from the parking lot before my accident but I knew that my wife and children would be there in the van. The problem too was that dusk was approaching and with it the closing of the park; I could already picture my name being engraved on the plaque of that year's Darwin Award.

Ultimately, I made it out of the woods and back to the car. When we got home, I took off my sneaker to examine my ankle; within minutes it had ballooned grotesquely and resembled a bruised grapefruit attaching my foot to my leg. A good friend from down the block donated a pair of crutches and my wife set up an appointment for me to see a doctor when the office would open next. I had endured sprained ankles in the past but never a broken one; the bright future that I had enjoyed earlier that day was suddenly dark with uncertainty.

To my surprise and relief, the x-rays came back negative. The doctor, despite the horrific appearance of my ankle, gave the typical recovery instructions and said that I should be healed in two weeks or so. I wasn't as certain as she was but I had hope that I would be able to get myself back on course. As it turned out, the journey back to running would be anything but smooth or straightforward.

My ankle did return to its normal size over the next two weeks but a grating pain persisted. I could walk without trouble but I was met with agony any time I tried to run or jump. Nearly four months passed with hardly any exercise and so the weight that I had lost once again returned. I felt stymied, defeated, and utterly mystified at my lack of recovery. I sought out a second opinion with a sports medicine doctor and wound up being referred for physical therapy.

My physical therapist Sue not only diagnosed the issue (a stubborn bone that refused to retract as it should have) but got me literally back on my feet; the despair of the summer melted away in a matter of moments as mobility and thus *activity* loomed ahead. Towards the end of October, I felt well enough to begin working out again but I didn't want to push myself too hard too soon; I had learned at least that much. Instead, I took advantage of a deal at the new Planet Fitness location that had opened and I signed up. I fell in love with their Cybex ArcTrainer machine and began a new workout regimen.

My first cardio workout on the ArcTrainer was on October 22nd, 2013—nearly nine months after I first started upon this adventure. I weighed in at 220.8 lbs and swore to myself that I would get under 200 pounds by October 22nd, 2014. It was a promise that I was determined to keep and one that ultimately spurred me through the next year.

I continued to enjoy my cardio workouts at the gym for the next few months but by March I had grown bored with the redundancy; I needed something more. It was then that I decided to tackle one of my bucket list challenges: undertaking a Century bike ride. The 100-mile ride had been a dream of mine since I was a kid but though I longed to complete it I never wound up doing so.

Determined to achieve both my weight loss and cycling goals, I dedicated myself to training with renewed fervor. By the time I set out upon my first training ride, I was already down to 206 lbs; it seemed inevitable that I would not only break the 200 lb. mark but would sail past it with ease. After three months of rigorous exercise, I completed a 110.26 mile bike ride; the day I did it, I still weighed 206 lbs.

I embarked upon only a few more bike rides during the summer of 2014 before returning to running. It was something that I was looking forward to but with tinges of reticence and fear; I was afraid that after putting so much effort into achieving that first 5K that I would somehow be incapable of repeating that success. To my surprise and relief, I was able to jump right into the Couch-to-10K program at the beginning of August. I completed the graduation 10K run on October 16th—less than a week before my year would be up; I weighed 201.8 lbs.

For all of the hard work that I had endured—all of the setbacks and tribulations, nothing compared with the disappointment that I felt during the four days following that run. I knew why I had yet to achieve my goal and I was angry, frustrated, and disappointed in myself. It was the first time I really held myself accountable and judged myself with unflinching honesty. For all of the success that I had enjoyed, I eroded part of it each and every time. It was gluttony that had stunted my weight-loss and in that moment I knew that I had to make a decision. I would have to put as much effort into changing my eating habits as I had into exercising; four days later, on October 20th, 2014, I weighed in at 199.4 lbs—my first time being below 200 in almost ten years.

Since that auspicious moment, I haven't looked back on the old lifestyle that I finally left behind. I haven't gone above the *195* pound mark let alone 200 since January of 2015 because of the changes that I made and the dedication that I have had towards my new way of life. I was tired of seeing pictures of people on Facebook who had lost weight, smiling and showing off their slimmed down, toned and tightened bodies. I was tired of the self-loathing that accompanied every poor eating and drinking decision and the pitiful perpetuity with which I engaged in these behaviors. I vowed to make the necessary changes not just to lose weight but to *keep it off*; ultimately, that's exactly what I did.

THE KEYS TO LOSING WEIGHT AND KEEPING IT OFF

Throughout my journey, I paid careful attention to what worked for me and what didn't. I have always been a proponent of self-analysis and so I utilized that perspective to help me to explore not just what led to my successes and failures but more importantly *why* those things did. That deep examination was critical because it helped me to understand my tendencies and how to overcome them or how to turn them into strengths. I had previously tried methods that worked for other people but failed without understanding why; only after critically assessing myself was I able to glean the knowledge that has at long last given me the success that I have sought.

These then are the keys to making positive changes that I have found that will help you not only embark upon your own journey of transformation but to maintain the fruits of your labors along the way.

EXCUSES, EXCUSES!

(HONESTY IS KEY)

The first key and single most important element of any personal transformation isn't motivation or dedication; it's not having a plan or a clear vision of the future. Instead, it's simply this: **self-honesty**. In order to succeed, you need to be honest with yourself not just about what you want and what your motivations are but about *why* you're in the position you find yourself in and why you *haven't* succeeded in the past. Until you're able to make this leap, you'll never enjoy a sustained, long-term metamorphosis.

The primary way in which we lie to ourselves is through excuse making; I know because I was an expert excuse-craftsman—a master of self-deception. I would convince myself that it was okay to have the four cookies that I wanted because I would skip having dessert later in the day; then, while enjoying dessert, I would reassure myself by saying that I would go for a run in the morning. Deep down, I *knew* that I was lying to myself but that deceit was necessary for me to continue to engage in the hedonistic lifestyle that I was enjoying.

150

I routinely told myself that I had enough stressors in my life, that something had to give, and that I would lose the weight and make the change "when the time was right." Now, looking back, I just shake my head in disbelief. By ignoring the very obvious signals that my body was sending me, I wound up making things *so much harder* by making my life "easier" in my mind by eating whatever I wanted without considering its impact on my overall health and failing to compensate for bad decisions through exercise and restraint. I lacked the confidence that was necessary to enact change and so I compensated for this by coddling myself and cloaking my battered ego in feeble rationalizations.

At one point or another, we all make excuses for ourselves. Sometimes it's a singular moment of self-sympathy while other times it's a full-blown pity party with all of the trimmings. Regardless, it's how we respond to those moments that ultimately determines whether or not we will get the results that we want in the long run. If they are infrequent, isolated incidents that do not recur then they are not harmful in the least; if however, they are indicative of a trend then a stern self-assessment is warranted.

Don't get me wrong—feeling sorry for yourself can actually be beneficial on occasion. I know that, for me, it serves as a moment of reset: I regret whatever decision it was that I made and I vow not to make it again. I adhere to certain self-imposed rules that help me to stay mentally and physically healthy and so when I invariably lapse and have a moment of weakness, it's important to me to be able to forgive myself and to move on—returning to the routine that has kept me healthy.

Sometimes we can be too hard on ourselves—something that proves to be self-defeating; we wind up psyching ourselves out and lose the confidence and motivation to continue along our uphill climbs towards healthier lives. More often we **simply make excuses** for our self-destructive behavior, erecting shields of indignant self-indulgence to protect our delicate egos and fragile self-esteems. What this is though is simply self-deception; we are lying to ourselves and are held unaccountable for our perfidy.

Excuses are arguably the number one reason people fail to achieve *anything* that they pursue. I know plenty of folks who hide behind the circumstances that they face and use those as an explanation for failure rather than looking at them simply as obstacles that need to be overcome. With fitness in particular there are a slew of universal excuses that I've heard people make. Here are just a few:

I'd like to but I just don't have the time.

I'm too old to change now.

Whenever I lose weight I just put it right back on.

It's just the way I am.

*I **can't** change.*

Just reading those has made my blood pressure rise. Self-serving statements like that fly freely from lips of people who should know better but who seem utterly incapable of recognizing one simple truth: they are all in denial. Each one of those utterances represents a reason in the minds of the utterers of why they haven't been able to accomplish their goals when in reality they are merely insipid rationalizations.

The most egregious of excuses are the ones about time and about being incapable of change. *SO* many people nowadays say "I just don't have the time" to do whatever it is that they're avoiding doing. I know that it might seem like a simple discrepancy in the words used but just <u>once</u> I would love for someone to say what they really mean: I'm choosing not to use my time to do _____.

That's really what it comes down to in nearly every case—not using the time available to engage in the activity in question. It might seem like a semantic issue but it's far deeper and more important than that; instead, it is a matter of honesty. People who say "I just don't have the time" are almost always lying to themselves. Obviously I cannot speak to the lives and lifestyles of every person out there but I can say with utter certainty that in a good many cases there *is* time for whatever it happens to be—it's just not utilized. Rising an hour early, going to bed an hour later, or choosing to exercise instead of (or perhaps while) watching an hour of television are all viable alternatives that debunk their temporal assertion.

Aside from being an issue of honesty, it's also a matter of *effort*. When it comes to exercise, cardio in particular, the primary excuse that people make is not having enough time; I call bullshit. Even if you have a multi-hour commute and a long day at the office each workday you can still find ways of engaging in cardio that you can build into the present infrastructure of your schedule. Electing to get off at an earlier stop to elongate the walk to the office, taking the stairs instead of the elevator wherever practical, or simply taking a stroll during lunch are three effective ways of accruing some much needed miles over the course of a workweek.

I have a buddy who gets into his office before seven most mornings and who leaves after ten or later on some of his longer days. I'm sure that he's exhausted when he gets home but he doesn't use that or his schedule as an excuse for avoiding cardio. Instead, he makes it a point to spend time on the treadmill multiple nights a week before going to bed at the expense of more sleep. **He *has* the time because he *makes* it.**

Present-day people are so weak-willed that it's pathetic. Few want to give up their indulgences, clutching to their laziness the way a toddler would grip a favorite blanket or stuffed animal. With even a modicum of self-evaluation it would be possible to adjust things in your schedule to make room for exercise if only you elect to do so. Sometimes it's as simple as watching television while on a treadmill or stationary bike but at worst it might mean rising a half an hour earlier or going to bed a half an hour later.

Sure that might be complicated for the single parent working two or three jobs to make ends meet…but there are two points of profound importance to be found in that example. The first is that most people *do not* fall into that category and lead comparatively far simpler lives. The second one is that, ironically, those are the exact type of people who *would* fight to make time for the things that are important to them; *they're* the ones who routinely forego sleep for study time.

I'll never forget a woman I went to graduate school with. It was easily the most stressful, time-consuming stretch of my life. I was living on Staten Island at the time, working and student teaching in Manhattan, and going to school in Brooklyn. Five days a week I was out of the house before five in the morning and on the ferry into the city, teaching until eleven or later, going to work in Midtown, then taking an express bus back to Staten Island so that I could get the car to drive to Brooklyn to attend class. I would get home after 9 or 10 each night, have dinner, and go to bed. My weekends were filled with lesson planning, essay, exam, and homework grading, textbook reading, and paper writing. In a word, I was swamped.

During those eight months I scarcely engaged in any sort of athletic endeavor and I ate *horribly*, again riding the wave of serotonin that helped me through each day. I felt sorry for myself and how "busy" I was until I learned about the life of a classmate. She was also in my graduate program but she was teaching full-time. She was a single parent with a physically and mentally disabled son and an elderly, invalid mother who were *both* under her care. *HER* day was stretched even thinner than mine was and yet, for exhausted as she was, she never once complained about her lot or her schedule; it was what it was and she did what she had to do.

I think of her every time I hear someone complain about not having the time—especially when they are home from work earlier in the day or routinely plow through television-watching marathons on the weekends. The answers are right in front of them but they are too blinded by their own self-absorbed pursuits of passive gratification to see that. They cannot even admit to themselves that they are making an unconscious (or not!) decision that is preventing them from engaging in a healthier, more fulfilling lifestyle.

When pressed, these people are also the ones who claim to be incapable of change. This one is perhaps even more infuriating than its predecessor because of how utterly asinine it is. We are *all* capable of change, regardless of age or environment. Some changes are more difficult than others to make and some will take far longer to stick but they are all almost universally possible. So few things in life are immutably permanent but people fail to recognize that with terrifying persistence.

To these people I say this: change the way you are. Stop making excuses for yourself and stop focusing on why you think you *can't* rather than on figuring out how you actually *can*. There is an epidemic of overuse and misuse of the word can't—one that cries out for another moment of honesty. When people say "can't" what they really mean is "won't." I challenge them (and you, if you count yourself among them) to say "I'm choosing not to" instead of "I can't" each time you reach for that excuse. It will be a moment of exhilarating but terrifying honesty…and also the first step towards enlightenment and self-improvement.

It might seem like an insignificant detail in the grand scheme of things when in actuality it is such a bold step that is absolutely *necessary* to succeeding. When we say that we *can't* we are hiding behind our environment or circumstances rather than exposing ourselves to potential judgment.

"Oh, I'd love to go for a bike ride but I *can't*—I have to run errands today."

"I wish I could but I *can't*—I'm going out to dinner later tonight."

"Thanks but I *can't*—I've just got too much going on right now."

Few people would question those excuses with the way that they're worded even though, in each situation, it really comes down simply to a juggling or restructuring of schedule.

"Oh, I'd love to go for a bike ride but I'm choosing not to—I have to run errands today."

"I wish I could but I'm choosing not to—I'm going out to dinner later tonight."

"Thanks but I'm choosing to do something else instead."

All of a sudden, there is an element of hurt feelings to be had here. Suddenly, with that simple change in verbiage, each proclamation becomes laden with ascriptions of value. Running errands is suddenly preferred over going bike riding—the biking inquisitor less important than the errands to be run. Instead of being confident and standing behind our decisions we *choose* instead to shrink and hide behind our excuses and circumstances.

In order to see the change we want to see we have to *be* that change—to be the embodiment of the behavior that we seek to engage in. We have to be honest with ourselves first and to hold ourselves accountable when we use faulty, contrived reasons for not doing something. Take a hard line with yourself when it comes to making excuses and you'll be surprised by how quickly and effectively you can begin making better decisions.

THE DECIDING FACTOR

(*REPLACING AND WITH OR*)

Being honest with ourselves and cutting back on excuses is critical to making better decisions but we still need to find ways of actually *making* those choices. It's one thing to be able to understand what you *should* be doing but it's another thing entirely to *do* it. Quite often, we think that we are being healthy and are doing the right things while being completely oblivious to our self-destructive decisions and the self-defeating consequences of our actions.

Case-in-point: me in 2014. I worked my *ass* off not just to complete that century bike ride but to start and finish an entire 10K program. You would think that I would have wasted away to nothing with the amount of exercise I did…but that didn't happen. Allow me to throw some numbers at you to put it into perspective:

Between January 1st, 2014 and October 20th, 2014—almost ten full *months*—I spent nearly ***12,000*** minutes doing cardio and covered more than 1,200 miles bipedally and by pedaling. I burned greater than 135,000 calories during that time and yet I managed to go from 213 pounds down to 199—a net loss of a measly 14 pounds. After my moment of honesty and epiphany, in a mere ten *weeks*, I lost another *13* pounds—almost exactly as much despite totals of only 2,600 minutes, 192 miles, and 36,000 calories burned.

Think about that for a second. I should have lost almost 40 pounds during those ten months yet the loss was miniscule by comparison. In contrast, I should have lost only 10 or so pounds during the final stretch of 2014 and instead lost *more*. The reason for both circumstances is the second most important element of personal transformation: **decision-making**.

I took a long hard look at myself towards the end of October and realized that, for every two steps forward that I took, I took one backwards. I was finally honest with myself and admitted that the decisions that I made repeatedly were not just stunting my progress but were hurting me in the long run. I was encouraged with my progress and had a tendency to *celebrate* each really long run or bike ride with a litany of treats; the harder I worked and further I went, the more I "rewarded" myself with unhealthy food.

And so it was that I admitted to myself that if I was ever going to attain not just the numerical goals that I wanted but also the long-term overall health ones then I needed to make some serious changes to the way I ate and drank as well as *what* I ate and drank. I realized that I wasn't merely consuming the wrong things but was doing so in *combination* and thus mass quantity. I looked at what I would have considered an average day during my time working in Midtown and realized that on most mornings, I would grab a doughnut *and* juice *and* a breakfast platter consisting of eggs *and* potatoes *and* several pieces of bacon. At lunch, I felt like I was making a "healthy" decision by eating at Subway but then I would order a full foot-long sandwich *and* a bag of chips *and* two cookies *and* finally a soda. Ultimately, I picked up on a disturbing trend in my decision making.

This moment of epiphany led me to the second key to losing weight: **replacing and with or**. The instant I changed my perspective I began to look at *everything* I ate and drank differently; suddenly, each item was imbued with value and importance that I had never considered before. I realized that I couldn't (or at least shouldn't) have them *all*. I became more conscious of what I was putting into my body and as a result I began making better decisions.

A quick analysis of your day would likely reveal numerous instances where you could swap *or* for *and*. If you have a sweet tooth like me and find yourself having some kind of treat and soda

163

with a meal why not consider choosing one over the other? They're both serving the same purpose so you'll still walk away with your sweetness yen sated if you wind up having only one of the two.

People seem to focus on the notion of cutting things out when really it's more effective to choose *when* you have the things that you enjoy; when it comes to poor eating habits in particular sometimes the best approach isn't to cut things out but rather to find substitutions. Rather than immediately cutting out the things that you enjoy but aren't necessarily good for you, why not take inventory of your unhealthy habits and ascribe value to them on a sliding scale?

I took a long, hard, critical look at the things that I ate and drank back in 2013 and I divided them up into things that I could live without easily and things that I derived a great deal of enjoyment from. By doing so, I realized that cookies, cake, ice cream, and candy were easy enough to kibosh but craft beer, burgers, and pizza were not. I'm also a sucker for potatoes so I was also unwilling to give up chips and fries.

I thought about what made me the happiest and I realized that I preferred the potato chips with a sandwich to the cookies or candy. I accepted the notion that I shouldn't have both and so I made a value judgment and decided to cut out the sweets. I was able to do this in one shot but there's no reason that anyone else should feel obligated to do so. Cutting back with the intention of fully cutting out is fine as long as, again, you're being honest with yourself. If seven months after you decide to cut back on your sweets you're still having the exact same amount (or more!) then you're not being as honest with yourself as you'd like to admit.

It was a lot easier for me to make changes to what I ate when I considered substitutions—going with "or" instead of "none at all"—and focused more on my eating habits than the particulars of what I ate. I like having something to drink with dinner other than water and, depending upon the night of the week, I enjoy having some type of craft beer. The problem was that I was having soda, juice, or something sweet and then having beer on top of it. I realized that simply by substituting the beer for the soda that I would be making progress. I eventually wound up cutting soda out almost completely, drinking water or flavored seltzer with dinner, and keeping craft beer for special occasions during the week simply because I was open to the idea of making substitutions rather than undergoing a complete upheaval of my lifestyle.

Going cold turkey is mostly an uphill battle so scaling down with the right mentality instead of cutting things out completely when you really don't want to will help to set you up for success rather than the inevitable relapse. Pay attention to your eating habits and consider making tradeoffs. There's no reason that you can't enjoy a few beers, some junk food, and other forms of empty calories but there's also no reason that you should feel the need to have them all in combination or to consume them in excess; moderation is a far more effective approach to making lifestyle changes than deprivation.

MODERATION NOT DEPRIVATION

(*WHY DIETING IS DOOMED FROM THE START*)

Weight loss can seem like an impossible feat attainable only by those with good fortune or some arcane abilities; in reality, it's something that comes with consistent good decision-making over a very long period of time. This latter point is of critical import because it speaks to why so many people fail in their efforts to slim down: they want the quick fix with the least amount of disruption to their ways-of-life. Unfortunately, any such fix is temporary and the rewards reaped evanescent at best; the weight will come back.

Aside from weight-loss pills and surgery, the primary quick fix that people seem to engage in is dieting; what these folks fail to realize though is that, in most cases, they're dooming themselves from the start. Dieting is great in theory because you're eliminating something that is deemed fattening or otherwise unhealthy. Where it falls apart though is in practice.

Dieters often deprive themselves of things that they like to eat and drink or eschew those things in lieu of healthier options. The problem is that, by its very nature, a diet is essentially a temporary change. People who follow a diet usually do so because of its popularity or its perceived benefits. They focus on the specifics of it (avoiding fats or carbohydrates, for example) but fail to embrace the spirit of it, which is about replacing the wrong foods and drinks with the right ones.

Over time, either when the dieters hit a wall with their weight loss or external circumstances have them yearning for the familiarity of their bad habits, they find themselves thinking about their comfort foods or drinks. The nature of dieting draws attention to the very thing that dieters are trying to distance themselves from! Eventually, they begin craving those things, inevitably slip and have some, feel guilty, and wind up abandoning the diet because of how bad they feel about themselves.

Simply put, the third key to losing weight and keeping it off is to **focus on moderation not deprivation**. At first, people who are depriving themselves feel great because they believe that they are engaging in healthy behavior. Over time though they get bored with what they are doing (again, in part because they perceive it as a temporary change), and they begin to miss the things that they've given up; they are focusing on *what* they are eating as opposed to *how* they are eating.

Certain types of calorie counters find themselves in the same situation as dieters. They have the right idea in terms of paying attention to how much food they're consuming but their diligence can become stressful if not an outright obsession. They adhere so strongly to their numbers that, when they inevitably err and go off-course, they feel intense umbrage and self-loathing. For some, this represents a path to the dark side of overindulgence and compensation.

Worse still are the folks who get caught up in the notion of eating so-called diet, low-calorie, or lite foods. They think that because the nutritional numbers appear to be positive that they can overindulge with no detriment to themselves. Unfortunately, what they fail to realize is that the flavor in low-fat snack foods still has to come from somewhere—often through an increase in sugar, salt, or, worse, some artificial additive; the same goes for sugar-free and even some low-salt items as well. Plowing through an entire package of low-fat cookies is even worse than having a handful or two of regular ones!

While it's true that you'll never lose weight eating only a steady diet of fatty foods and drinking empty calories, the opposite situation is just as likely to fail without the proper mindset. Can you imagine eating only tiny portions of vegetables or the same chicken, broccoli, and brown rice for the rest of your life and drinking only water? If so then that's great because you've already won half the battle. Me? I feel as if I'm like most people: I need my burgers, pizza, and beer!

I tried giving up all of the things that I loved that are bad for me and you know what happened? I was <u>miserable</u>. Guess what ensued? You got it: not only did I return to those comfort foods, I went overboard in my consumption of them. When I finally embraced those things and began considering which among them I preferred the most I found a healthier mindset and success in my weight loss goals, which leads me to the next point: **allow for an occasional indulgence!**

We're not robots. We endure cravings, hankerings, and desires for things that we shouldn't have. There are those among us who give in way too frequently to those wants and those who struggle always to avoid them but the ones who are happiest are those who concede on occasion. Remember—it's easy to lose sight that your goals are long-term ones that will affect your life and lifestyle and will thus take time to become the norm. As such, errors in judgment or slip-ups are easier to absorb if they're viewed as just that: single mistakes that will not be repeated routinely. As long as you are eating better and eschewing the less healthy treats <u>more often than not</u> then not only will you likely be more successful, you'll be happier too! Have that once-in-a-while soda or cookie as long as it remains just that—once in a while; be moderate and you won't find yourself feeling desperate.

My problem was that after every great workout came a great setback in the form of overindulgence. I was eradicating my progress and making it infinitely harder on myself to stay motivated with my workouts because I kept eating and drinking the wrong things <u>all the time</u>. I used them as motivation during many of my workouts when I should have been viewing them more as an occasional reward. I also failed to consider just how bad some of this stuff was for me and why I even wanted it in the first place.

UNDERSTAND WHAT'S GOING INTO YOUR BODY AND WHY

Making the right eating decisions is a necessary but mystifying step for a lot of people in trying to lose weight; **understanding what it is that we are actually eating and why we are eating it** is thus the fourth key to our transformations. People look at this step as being something so seemingly simple and yet so damn hard to do. They wonder why they have such a difficult time doing something that in theory shouldn't even warrant a second thought; the answer, in part, is literally all around us.

Fast food restaurants are *everywhere*. Think about how many you pass throughout the day. How many are within a few minutes of work or home? How expensive is the food that they're offering? In many cases, these places are offering food that has been chemically engineered in one way or another to get you to want more. The prices are usually ridiculously low because these places make money based off of quantity not quality (like many macrobreweries).

For many folks, the temptation and convenience of these places are too much to resist; ignoring their siren songs is a Sisyphean endeavor. After all, the food tastes great and it's extremely economical so why avoid it? The ubiquity of these restaurants leads to unparalleled access and their inimitable pricing leads invariably and inevitably to excessive consumption.

The sequence that leads people to these eating lifestyles is simple: they feel like they're hungry and they want something that they believe tastes good and so they keep eating until they believe that they are full. There are several reasons why people overeat but when it comes to fast food or food that is chemically engineered it's what goes into the food itself that can create the impulse. Certain additives trick the brain into thinking that the food tastes a certain way or that you want to eat more of it than you otherwise would. It's what creates that seemingly insatiable appetite sensation when you're plowing through that chain pizza or burger and fries and are then surprised by how much you were able to put away.

Foods that are high in fat, sugar, and salt all have a tendency to taste good but they are also the least healthy for us. They are also hardly limited to fast food restaurants and producers of guilty pleasures. I used to love ordering the specialty burgers at places like Applebee's and T.G.I.Friday's until I happened to scope out how much fat and sodium went into them. In some cases, the totals for that one burger—not even counting the fries or ketchup—would exceed the total recommended amount for *the entire day*!

Being more knowledgeable about what we eat is only half the battle though; understanding *why* we eat when and how we do is arguably even more important. Too often, we eat for the wrong reasons when we really don't need to. Boredom is arguably the primary culprit but emotions play a factor too. How often do we reach for some feel-good food when we're in a heightened state of anger, sadness, or elation? How many times are we sitting in a meeting or in class, bored to tears, when we're suddenly struck with an inexplicable urge to consume some sort of salty or sugary treat?

We often eat because we *think* we are hungry when in reality we aren't and we also consume well beyond the point that our bodies are full. Perhaps the most helpful way to avoid doing both of these things is to think of our bodies as machines—cars, for our purposes. Most drivers fill up their cars with gasoline when they're running low; none, presumably, go to the pump and ask for twenty gallons when the tank holds only twelve. Those who own higher performing vehicles too consider better fuel options for their cars because they are more efficient.

Why then shouldn't we look at our bodies as similar machines? Food after all is simply our fuel and yet we treat it oftentimes as something more—something that it doesn't *have* to be. When your body needs fuel it will tell you; when it's had enough, you'll also know. The problem is that we often misinterpret signals from our brain as hunger and ignore or fail to wait for the ones that tell us to stop eating.

Simply put, we eat because we *want* to—because doing so provides us with pleasure—and so we tend to eat the wrong things and too much of them. By disentangling the pleasure aspect of food from its fueling purpose we are able to make better decisions about what to eat and when. That's not to say that we shouldn't enjoy what we eat but rather that we shouldn't use that as the primary motivation in eating.

We also have a tendency to eat until we have emptied our plates rather than until we are full; it's what makes buffets and smorgasbords so dangerous to our waistlines. There is an undeniable psychological element to eating—a sense of completion and the requisite pleasure that is derived from a job well done—that accompanies an empty plate. It comes down to our brains being deceived: put a large piece of chicken on a smaller plate with enough vegetables to cover it and we are sated when we're done; take that exact same meal and put it on a plate that is twice as large and we walk away still feeling hungry because our perception is that we didn't eat that much.

The trick then is to be aware of the fact that the size of the dish the food is served on can have as much of an impact on our appetite as the dish itself and to consider where the calories in these foods are coming from.

BE CALORIE *COGNIZANT* & AWARE OF SERVING SIZES

Being a hardcore calorie counter can be as stressful as engaging in an extensive diet but **having at least a cursory awareness of the amount and type of calories in the things we put into our bodies** is the fifth key to losing weight; I think of this as being *calorie cognizant*. Limiting the proportion of calories that come from fat and carbohydrates will help you to slim down faster than merely looking at the overall number. Part of being conscious of calories is also recognizing serving sizes and understanding how they can be used as a secret weapon of sorts in your quest to slim down and to be healthier.

There's nothing wrong with eating too much of a healthy thing but too often we over-consume the foods that we should have less of. A helpful starting point for limiting our intake of the bad stuff is considering serving sizes and portions. When it comes to the latter, the formula is simple: eat more of the healthy food on our plates and less of the unhealthy. Just because we are given an excessive amount of food at a restaurant does not mean that we should eat it in a single sitting. There's nothing wrong with asking for a takeaway container with your meal and then dividing the food in half. It's an economical move because you're doubling the number of meals you're getting for your money and you're drastically reducing the amount of calories that you're consuming in a single sitting.

When it comes to serving sizes, there's a certain sense of arbitrariness in their determination. Some people swear by them but I find them to be merely a useful starting point or guideline. Really it's the accompanying nutritional information that matters but the numerical value of the serving size can be helpful in its own right.

Here's an example. Let's say you want a snack and you have a box of Entenmann's Frosted Pop'ems and a bag of Pepperidge Farm Goldfish crackers in front of you. A quick look at the Nutrition Facts for each reveals the following: a serving size of the Entenmann's consists of four Frosted Pop'ems at a cost of 320 calories and 23 grams of fat, 14 of which are saturated (the equivalent of 70% of the recommended Daily Value).[51] The Pepperidge Farm serving size consists of 55 Cheddar Goldfish pieces at a cost of 140 calories and 5 grams of fat, only 1 of which is saturated.[52] The percentage of calories from fat for the Pop'ems is roughly 65% and only 32% for the Goldfish.

With those numbers before you, which would you choose? Again, it depends upon what your motivation is. If you're hungry and you want a snack that will be more filling then the Goldfish would be the way to go because there's more in a single serving, it'll cost you less in terms of fat and calories, and it'll take you longer to eat! You could probably fit all four Pop'ems into your mouth at one time and be hungry ten minutes later. If you wanted a *treat* and were willing to substitute in something far healthier later on then the Pop'ems wouldn't be as big of a deal…as long as you don't wind up having them *and* another unhealthy treat to fill you up.

Many people find it easier to control their portion sizes when they eat at home but find it nearly impossible to do so when they go out to eat. It's true that many restaurant chains offer large portions for the money spent on them but sometimes they go way overboard providing enough food to feed two or *more* people on one plate. Splitting an appetizer platter, downing a full burger and fries, and then having dessert at one of these restaurants often means not just exceeding up your entire day's allotment of calories, fat, and salt but potentially ***doubling*** it.

Invoking our mantra of moderation once again, there's nothing wrong with having some of the aforementioned things but it is far better to divide what you order into at least two portions because you'll likely still be sated, you'll give your body more time to process everything, and you'll get more out of your meal and for your money. The simplest way to do this is to ask for a takeout container when you place your order. Most restaurants will do this without a problem so there should be no embarrassment associated with such a request; after all, the employees there aren't the ones who have to deal with the impact of *your* eating and drinking decisions.

Even then there are times that I really crave a delicious but dietarily-deadly burger that I'll want to finish in one sitting and so I make adjustments during the day to allow for it (this is where the *or* comes into play in a more macroscopic sense). If I know that I'm going to be going out to dinner then I'll eschew empty calories during the day and make sure that I do enough cardio that day, the day before, or the day after to offset the astronomical caloric intake that will occur. This way, I'm still getting what I want but in a more reasonable fashion.

I also view a dinner out as a treat unto itself whereas I used to view it as an ordinary meal. At most places like the aforementioned national restaurant chains though the calorie counts are devastating—far higher than anything I would have cooked for myself at home. It would be nearly impossible to eat there with regularity and consume the best-tasting-but-worst-for-you-foods and not wind up gaining weight (among other more serious health issues). Ergo, I now put such an outing in the same mental category as craft beer, soda, and sweets: an occasional treat that I ultimately do not need but simply would like to have.

My sweet tooth is my biggest weakness but I have managed to turn it into a strength simply by altering my mindset and knowing myself well. I know that I am weak-willed in the presence of aromatic, freshly-baked goods or damn near anything that's frosted. As a result, I do my best to avoid them almost entirely, substituting other things that scratch that sweetness itch without destroying my hard work.

I knew that I had finally turned a corner when in 2013 Halloween came and I didn't have a single piece of candy. Not one! And this was with two adorable, full-fledged trick-or-treaters in the house who came back absolutely flush with sweet swag. I knew that it was a slippery slope for myself and that even one taste would likely lead to more empty wrappers in the garbage. The most surprising part was how *easy* the decision was and with what little effort it took to adhere to it. Simply by looking at the calories involved and the accompanying serving size, I was able to recognize the value that certain foods had over others and to admit to myself that some things that I used to love simply weren't worth it; in the end, the effort that it would take to burn off their calories far exceeded the enjoyment that they would have given me.

CREATE A CALORIC DEFICIT

(*KNOW YOUR METABOLIC RATE!*)

On paper, the trick to losing weight is simple: your body needs to burn off more calories than it takes in; this is called **creating a caloric deficit** and is our sixth key to weight loss. This can be achieved in a variety of ways but the two most common would be by reducing the number of calories consumed or exercising to burn off more calories. It appears elegant in principle but it's harder than it seems because of the complexities involved with calories and how they affect our bodies. Calories from fat and carbohydrates affect the body differently than those gleaned from protein. The time of day that they are consumed can have an impact as can your overall metabolic rate, which will determine how quickly and efficiently they are burned off.

According to Under Armour's My Fitness Pal website, "Your BMR (Basal Metabolic Rate) is an estimate of how many calories you'd burn if you were to do nothing but rest for 24 hours. It represents the minimum amount of energy needed to keep your body functioning, including breathing and keeping your heart beating."[53] While it is a more complicated affair than described, taken at its most basic level, the BMR can serve as an invaluable tool for weight loss. It's hardly a fail-safe calculation and there are other more complex and time-consuming ones that you can do but for me BMR served and continues to serve its purpose as a motivating factor in my fitness and weight loss pursuits.

A lot of conjecture exists regarding the efficacy and accuracy of calorie burning calculations and metabolic rates (both Basal Metabolic and its cousin Resting Metabolic) and I believe that there's something to be said for that. I wouldn't rely on *any* of these calculations as being 100% accurate and so instead I choose to use them simply as a starting point; this is where their true value lies. Knowing the general information about them and being able to calculate your own number will give you a loose guideline upon which to build your weight-loss efforts.

Essentially, your BMR or RMR gives you an idea of the minimum number of calories that your body will burn in a given day. The actual number is something that I'm sure fluctuates daily because of various environmental and physiological changes that invariably occur (i.e. stress levels, whether or not you have a cold, how long you go between meals, etc.) but the general number provides you with invaluable information. When I began working out, I had calculated my daily calorie requirement to be almost 2,300 calories. I figured that, at worst, there could be a discrepancy of a few hundred calories between that number and what my body actually needed; that's where my working out came into play. I knew that as long as I didn't exceed that particular number *and* I burned off several hundred calories then I would reduce the chance that I would exceed my daily allotment of calories and thus put on more weight.

When I began thinking in terms of my BMR or RMR I was suddenly, almost magically able to put more consideration into the quality of the food I was eating. I remember when then-Mayor Bloomberg enacted a law that required establishments in New York City to display calorie counts for foods. I suppose it had a major impact on the eating habits for some but for me, I would just chuckle at how bad the chicken fingers and fries were that I was about to eat; *NOW*, with a reference point, I can appreciate the toll that such calorie-rich meals have on my body.

I find myself to be more inclined nowadays to take a quick peek at the nutritional facts label or to look up the information for restaurants online than I once was because it helps me to make a value decision. Sometimes I will still opt for a breakfast sandwich that's bad for me but most times I *won't* go for something if it exceeds certain thresholds for calories and fat that I have set up for myself. Other things like pizza and burgers grilled at home receive no calorie considerations whatsoever because those are my cheat treats and so I allow for them by following the earlier advice of making tradeoffs and substitutions; when I have pizza and the like, that serves *as* my treat rather than the supplemental things that I used to enjoy with it.

Still, there is immense value in having an idea of the number of calories that your body needs for its day-to-day activities and to maintain its exact weight. Use this knowledge to find the best path for yourself towards your ultimate weight goal, either by cutting back on your calories (particularly those from fat) and/or by upping your activity level. Also, it's easier to look at your calorie deficit goals as weekly ones than it is daily because it gives you more leeway with absorbing mistakes and thus more time to atone for them.

Having a number in mind in terms of what my body needed provided me with immense psychological benefits. Suddenly, that burger that I wanted to order that had 1,300 calories and tons of fat didn't seem as desirable as it once did when I realized that I'd be eating up more than half of my daily allotment in one sitting. Knowing that it would take more than 90 minutes of intense cardio at the gym or a comparable run outside *just to burn off the one burger* gave me the strength and conviction that I needed to make better decisions.

CREATE AN ENVIRONMENT THAT IS CONDUCIVE TO CHANGE

(*EXAMPLES, EXCUSES, AND EXECUTION*)

Though our transformations begin inwardly we are undoubtedly affected by our environments; we can set ourselves up for success by surrounding ourselves with the right people. If you think about it there are really three types of friends: the yes friends, the no friends, and the truly honest friends. We seek the input of the yes friends when we want to do something we probably shouldn't and the counsel of the no friends when there's something that we *don't* want to do. We value the advice of our closest friends the most because they are usually the only ones who are wholly honest with us but all too often we fail to make use of that trait when it comes to bad behaviors.

People who are weak-willed often find their lives filled with enablers—people who tell them exactly what they want to hear and who fail to put them in their place when they do something detrimental to themselves. It's easy to lose oneself in a cushion of ego-stroking and it becomes infinitely harder to listen to the honest assessments of well-meaning truthful friends when the voices of the enablers drown them out. If you're going to succeed in your mission of self-improvement then you're going to have to minimize the presence and influence of the people who will steer you wrong; the seventh key then is to **create an environment that is conducive to fostering positive change**.

Eventually, the goal is to turn yourself into a machine of self-accountability but until then it doesn't hurt to have a support system in place to help you to recover from some bad decisions. You want someone who is going to be compassionate but firm in telling you that you made a mistake. They need to be encouraging but unwilling to accept any excuses; they have to be able to tell you when you've messed up **and you have to be willing to listen**.

Let's say you come back from a great run or bike ride and you want to crack open a can of soda and a bag of cookies. If your significant other can fill the aforementioned role for you then that's great because (s)he can simply shake his or her head and guide you out of your moment of weakness towards a better decision. If you slip up and tell him or her about it afterwards then they should be equally able to say, "That's okay but you know you shouldn't have done that, right? Just make sure that you make the right decision next time."

If, however, that significant other is the one who is getting you the cookies and soda in the first place then you might have to look elsewhere for guidance and support. The point is that having the proper support system in place can lead us to success while having the *wrong* one will invariably lead to our downfalls. Make sure that you know the people in your life well enough to decide whether or not they can play active roles in your metamorphosis.

It can help immensely to have people in your corner that are not only supportive but emblematic of the change that you seek to make. It could be as simple as someone who has lost and kept off a considerable amount of weight or someone who demonstrates rigorous discipline and consistency in eating or exercise habits. Seek out others who have attained the success that you are after (whether it is simply weight loss or something more ethereal) and, when possible, ask them about their personal journeys. Listen carefully to what they say and see what resonates with you; try to identify commonalities between their tales and assess whether they have any relevance to you and your path. Don't be afraid to be a little bit jealous or envious of their success provided you use it as motivation to fuel your own hunt; there is a world of difference between wanting what someone else has and thinking "I can do that too" and looking at that person's success and thinking "I'll *never* be able to do that…"

You must also realize that what worked for *them* might not work for *you* even if you think that it sounds feasible; they might have a very different outlook on eating and exercising than you do. This is the time for brutal honesty and ruthless candor with yourself. Think about whether or not you are still making excuses for yourself and, if you are, then find a way to own up to them so that you can leave them behind as relics of an unhealthy era.

Of course, all of the examples and self-studying will take you only so far; after that comes execution. You need to envision the change that you want to make and then begin to map out the route that will take you there. Don't expect that initial plan to be *the* one— use it as a starting point. It would be foolish and self-defeating to think that you will not deviate on your journey; when you finally reach the top, you'll look back and see that your road was hardly a straight line but rather a meandering one that doubled back on itself, went off-course, and zig-zagged but ultimately veered back on track and led you to the summit.

Beware placing too much stock in any one example—you might wind up empowering that person too much thereby inadvertently shifting the onus and agency over *your* change onto *them*. This is what seems to happen on a lot of these weight loss-oriented reality shows: the participants rely too much on the structure and the support essentially putting it upon on their coaches to be their sole source of motivation. Then, once everything ends, they fall immediately back into their old ways simply because they never really made a change in the first place. Make sure that your paragon of personal improvement is simply a good model to consider and not someone that you follow absolutely.

Having great examples to follow is a critical component of any personal transformation but sometimes you're given the opportunity to set that example yourself. A simple way to do this is to take ownership of your eating and drinking habits in social settings. I always thought it was strange that a friend of ours would pass on snack foods and appetizers when we hosted parties at our home until I began losing weight and changed my outlook. Suddenly

I realized the value of everything that I consumed and understood that sometimes it just wasn't worth wasting part of my daily allotment on something **simply because it was there**; it turns out that he employed the same philosophy to his eating and drinking decisions.

I have noticed especially that at particularly festive affairs like weddings and sporting events that people will eat and drink things that they would otherwise pass over for something they enjoy to a far greater degree, particularly when it comes to beer. Many a craft beer fanatic seems to succumb to this notion that they must drink a less favored macrobrew simply because it is the only perceived option; what they fail to consider is that *not* drinking or waiting until later to drink something better is always a choice. I understand that some people want to drink or eat specifically because of their location (again, usually at a gathering or sporting event) but doesn't it seem frivolous for that to be the sole or even primary factor that determines their drinking and eating habits?

It comes down to being comfortable with *yourself* and adhering to your own belief system rather than worrying about the perception of others. To date, no one has ever approached me about not drinking at a wedding reception, birthday party, casual party, or sporting event and even if they did, what would it matter to me? *I'M* the one who has to deal with the repercussions of my decisions and the physical effects of what I eat and drink—not *them*, so why should I give any consideration to someone else's negative opinion about my behavior? The bottom line is not to eat or drink something because you feel you have to and to set your own example if there isn't a good one to follow.

GOOD FOR THE BODY

(*FINDING THE RIGHT TYPE OF EXERCISE*)

Eating right is crucial to losing weight and increasing overall health but there is no substitute for a solid exercise regimen. It helps to keep not only your body functioning smoothly but your mind as well. My time at the gym or when I go out running is often the only quiet moment I have for myself during the day. It's an opportunity to get away from all of the stress that's been accumulating and to help to expel whatever negativity has been building up.

Most people avoid working out because they say or they think that it's too hard. They say that because they've gotten so drastically out of shape (much like I had!) and they're embarrassed and disheartened by how heavily they're breathing after some meager calisthenics or a jaunt on the treadmill. They see others bounding past them and they grow dejected believing that they will never be able to attain that level of fitness (so why even try, right?)

The problem and the solution are one in the same: they just haven't found the right cardio activity for *them*. Everyone needs a starting point but too often we feel compelled to dive headlong into the deep end rather than allow ourselves a moment to dip our toes in and get acclimated to the fitness pool. Running wound up being my key to personal victory but only because of the gradual pace and structure that the Couch-to-5K program afforded me. I supplemented this with the Cybex ArcTrainer machine at the gym but really running is what's kept the fire burning inside of me to challenge myself and to keep working out hard.

The trick is to commit to the *idea* of cardio first before you start trying to do too much too soon; **finding the *right type* of exercise for you** then is the eighth key to losing weight. Test out a program like Couch-to-5K even if you despise running; its structure and pace could prove to be the difference for you much like it was for me. If not, then perhaps trying a video program like the ones offered by Beachbody. I thoroughly enjoyed completing the P90X program but there are a few caveats worth considering. For one, I have an extensive history of working out and began that program already familiar with the types of exercises and the effort necessary to finish everything; if you've never stepped foot in a gym before or are extremely unfamiliar with working out in general then you would have to consider taking it very, *very* slow so as to avoid unnecessary injury.

Pursuant to the previous warning, I must advise against succumbing to the allure of programs like the Insanity workout and other extreme exercise collections if you're not used to working out. They are mostly excellent programs and you will undoubtedly gain strength and lose weight with them…but you're also risking serious harm to yourself if your body isn't properly primed. Most of the results that purportedly come from completing the program actually stem from completing it *several times* AND following a meal plan that comes packaged with the program oftentimes with the additional requirement of purchasing supplemental materials like shakes; jumping into an intense, rigorous exercise program not only sets you up with a chance of injuring yourself—it also causes you to set unrealistic expectations for yourself.

Realistic expectations and attainable goals are absolutely critical to success; telling yourself that you want to be able to bench press 1,000 lbs a year from now is more modest than saying you'll do it in a month but if it's not feasible then why set such a high benchmark for yourself? When I first started running back in 2013, the goal was to complete a 60 second run (*seconds!!!*); my longest run came less than two years later on Martin Luther King, Jr. Day:

14.20 miles in two and a half hours. I **_never_** thought that I'd be able to do 14 minutes let alone 14 *miles* but I did and part of the reason why is that I built up my expectations gradually.

It's good to have what I think of as "ultimate" goals—the things that you dream about one day accomplishing—because they can be incredibly motivating. In order to make them work for you though you have to make sure that they are not the *only* goals that you have and, just as importantly, that they don't remain at the forefront of your mind until you're drawing closer to achieving them. For more than half of my life I dreamed of completing a 100-mile bike ride. When I finally did, it took me exactly five bike rides to do it—four training rides and then the 110.26 mile ride. Those results seem impossible but the reason why they're true is because of my timing: I decided to start my training when I was finally in really good shape. Every other time I considered it I was sedentary and sluggish; at those points it remained an evanescent dream just beyond the reach of my fingertips.

The point is to dream big but to realize that it will take many, *many* smaller steps to lead you ultimately to your personal pinnacle. I had put in thousands of hours lifetime on my bike to accrue the knowledge and experience that ultimately helped me to succeed and hundreds of hours or more engaging in other cardio leading up to the moment when I knew I was finally ready to tackle my challenge. As it was, my penultimate ride wound up being 72.22 miles but that was supposed to be the day that I finished the Century. Technically, I failed in my first attempt but then came back twenty days later to do nearly *forty miles better*; being prudent in my mental approach and physical preparation allowed me to succeed but it was also simply because I loved what I was doing and never viewed it as arduous work.

That penultimate point speaks also to why I successfully completed the P90X program but failed ultimately to keep the weight off: my mental approach was not on par with my physical preparation. I was motivated by the people in the videos because I identified with them but what separated us was my inability to think beyond the 90 days and to set a longer term goal for myself. I stressed myself out by looking at the physical changes they were able to make and thinking that I could do it too without considering the extent of the work such an improvement would take; I failed to commit to a *lifelong* changing process and focused instead on the ephemeral short-term one.

Now, don't get me wrong, it can be both encouraging and deflating to look at pictures or videos of people who are incredibly fit from working out. More often than not though the folks who grace the covers of fitness magazines or who appear on television with ripped abs and massive arms have advantages that most of us do not. Sometimes it's simply genetics but other times it is access to personal trainers or the freedom in schedule to work*out* for hours on end when most folks are work*ing*.

These Adonises and Aphrodites *can* serve as positive inspiration but only to a point; if you think that you'll look like them in only a matter of weeks or months and with minimal effort you'll find that you're sadly mistaken. The dietary dedication and fitness fidelity that is necessary not just to attain that type of physique but to *maintain* it over a long period of time is intense. That's not to say that it isn't worth striving for but washboard abs should be only a part of what drives you.

The most critical mental steps that you can take towards achieving your transformation are understanding and adopting the notion that such a monumental change is akin to marathon running and not a sprint. It's something that should take you not just a long time to implement but arguably your entire *life* to uphold. Banging out a few sets of crunches in between fast food meals isn't going to cut it—you're going to have to make some serious changes in the way you eat and to your activity level, some of which will take weeks or months to enact or adjust to.

Give yourself a timeline but make sure that it's broad enough to allow for the inevitable plateaus that you will hit and will have to overcome. Saying that you want to lose ten pounds in two weeks is admirable but giving yourself two *months* to achieve that goal is far more reasonable. You might still lose that weight in less time but then you'll be ahead of the game and will feel even more empowered; if on the other hand you failed to reach that mark in your self-imposed short timeframe then you would feel defeated. Set yourself up for success by giving yourself a fair amount of time to lose an equally plausible amount of weight.

Knowing yourself and your habits is another crucial aspect to improving your chances of slimming down successfully. Once you're committed to the idea of losing weight *somehow* you then need to adhere to a schedule. Some people are great in the morning and can fit in their workouts before work; other people do better at night before bed. There are folks who prefer to exercise in the comfort of their home and others still who need to be in a gym to perform. A little self-analysis will go a long way and will help remove some potentially obvious and avoidable obstacles from your path.

Setting your alarm an hour early so that you'll work out before you leave might sound great but if you're someone who hits the snooze button a half dozen times before dragging yourself out of bed and over to the coffeemaker then you might want to consider a different time of day. I take a while to get going in the morning so that's not the best time for me but though I'm up late most nights I dislike exercising *too* late because the adrenaline rush winds up keeping me awake for far too long. Instead, I try to squeeze my workouts in during the day when possible or as early in the evening as I can.

When scheduling your workouts you need also to consider what will help you to maximize your effort and thus your results. Using a program like P90X or T25 provides you with the convenience of working out at home but it is useful only if you are disciplined enough to bring it each and every time. Some people know that they will not work out hard at home and so they go to the gym only to half-ass it *there* instead.

Whether you're walking on a treadmill at the gym, riding your bike outdoors, or striding along an elliptical machine at home you absolutely _must_ put maximum effort into what you're doing—otherwise, what's the point of working out? I can't tell you how many people I see who are clearly dedicated to losing weight but who are oblivious to their dearth of effort. They stroll along at a snail's pace on the treadmill holding onto the sides or pedal lethargically on the stationary bikes while either reading a magazine or fiddling with their phones. Others still seem to space out in the middle of lifting weights where they are *clearly* using way too little weight but are oblivious to it because they're not even paying attention to what they are doing.

The bottom line is this: if you're putting your time and your energy into losing weight and improving your life then do yourself a favor and commit to maximum effort ***every time***. If you're not sure of how to perform a particular exercise and you're at the gym then just ask a trainer. If you're trying to navigate a set of exercises at home and are confounded then hop onto YouTube and scope out some video instructions. User Scooby1961 has tons of invaluable information on his YouTube channel that he conveys in a straightforward, easy-to-follow fashion otherwise there are myriad other reputable websites that can help you to figure it out including Men's Health, Men's Fitness, Shape.com, and BodyBuilding.com

The only person who knows how hard you're working is *you* so be tough on but honest with yourself when you're working out. It's okay to take it slow every now and then but *only* if you're bringing it with consistent intensity every other time. If you're not capitalizing on your efforts then you won't be maximizing your gains; it can be difficult to stay mentally sharp and committed but that's where your support network should come into play!

Getting motivated to make a big life change is almost always easier than staying motivated. There are many little tricks and mind games that you can play with yourself to keep your morale high but nothing beats keeping an eye on the future. Having a variety of goals keeps you focused on moving forward rather than stalling or plateauing in your efforts. It helps also to propel you forward by turning your attention towards the things to come rather than allowing you to become fixated upon the potential struggles of the present or the mistakes of the past.

Falling into a rut can be a killer when it comes to your fitness routine and so an easy remedy is simply to **have three attainable goals at all times: an objective, numerical weight-based goal, a subjective personal aesthetic goal, and some type of physical challenge**; these goals represent the ninth key not just to losing weight but to keeping it off. During my transformation, I focused on the first and third more so than the second because I had no idea of what my body was going to look like at a lower weight. I didn't want to set myself up for disappointment with visions of ripped pecs and titanium abdominals. Instead, I used the 200 lb. benchmark as my motivator and a multitude of running challenges most of which were built into the C25K and C210K programs like the culminating graduation runs.

Again though whatever your goals happen to be you have to keep them reasonable and attainable. It's okay to desire that six or eight pack but break it down into smaller, component steps. Maybe you can shoot for losing your spare tire or fitting into a certain pair of pants first en route to your model-like figure. You'll derive more satisfaction from the journey and when you look back you'll be able to appreciate each of those milestones rather than being perpetually disappointed by your incremental progress towards something that might ultimately be unattainable anyway.

Weight-wise, it's great to have a number in mind but be sure that it suits your body type. I weighed between 150 and 160 pounds in high school but I don't think I could possibly attain the same number now even though I'm basically the same height. Back then, I wasn't as healthy in my habits and I was far more active than I could ever be now. I'm happy at my current weight and don't want to get psyched out trying to reach a lower but potentially unsustainable number.

I wouldn't stress the challenge aspect too early on but as you begin to progress and excel in your cardio workouts then it's not only advisable but almost necessary to have some kind of proverbial mountain to climb. It can be distance- or time-based or something as simple as "I want to be able to run a mile without breathing heavily." You'll work that much harder when you're putting your energy towards something tangible and specific and you'll appreciate the end result that much more. The last thing that you want to do is feel like you're slogging through your workouts with no end in sight.

One way to avoid the latter is to keep a log of all of your cardio workouts. I mentioned being a sucker for lists in the beer section so it should come as no surprise that I maintain one for exercising as well. Being a numbers guy, I keep a spreadsheet rather than a database so that I can perform calculations and analyze the output of my workouts. To date, I've spent 37,000 minutes covering more than 3,200 miles by self-propulsion and burning roughly 430,000 calories in the process. I use MapMyRun and MapMyRide to log my runs and rides, mapping them out and then adding the data to my spreadsheet.

Not only do I find this record keeping fun—I also find it to be a source of great motivation and sense of accomplishment. I love going out for a run now and scoping out the time as I shut off the stopwatch app. Then, when I map out the route on the aforementioned websites, I'm even more proud of the miles that I've covered. It reinforces how hard I've been working and it drives me to do even better the next time; if I had a bad workout then I can simply look at the plethora of *good* ones that I've had to remind myself that it's merely a temporary flub and that I will get back on track again.

Sometimes we can push ourselves too hard or set the bar too high when it comes to working out. The danger in doing so is physical (as we risk injury) but mental and emotional as well; the sting of even a single failure can wipe out the confidence gained from dozens of successful workouts. I hit a few walls during my Couch-to-5K program where I was unable to sustain a running pace for the given amount of time. Most of the times I *was* able to do better the next time out but there were a few instances where it was still a struggle.

The challenge of such a set of circumstances is not to allow what truly is a temporary setback to transform into a seemingly insurmountable obstacle. It could be your body telling you that you need to take a step back or simply the universe saying that it's not your time. Whatever the case might be, take it as an opportunity for some reflection and self-analysis to see whether or not there are any specific reasons why you're not succeeding. Focus on a different challenge or type of exercise for a little while to allow both your body and your ego to recover and then give it another shot. Few such obstacles are impossible to overcome and as such it's simply a matter of finding the correct combination of circumstances to move you past them; be a problem-solver and you'll enjoy a much smoother ascent to weight-loss nirvana.

Listening to your body is also of the utmost importance, especially when you find yourself struggling either to make progress in your efforts or to maintain them; this simple act was the unsung hero of my transformation because it enabled me to stay healthier longer. I'm a very driven person who needs little if any motivation from anyone else or an external source to go after the things that I want to pursue. My problem is one of going too hard, too soon, and for too long. When it came to the Couch-to-5K program though I knew that I wanted *sustained* success in the long run as opposed to quick fix gratification of my fungible, capricious goals. As a result, I listened to my body when it was telling me that I was pushing too hard and went to greater lengths both to prepare for and to recover from my runs.

Regardless of my athletic activity, I stretch and prime myself ahead of time. I recognize that there are two schools of thought when it comes to stretching but I personally can't understand why you *wouldn't* warm up even a little bit. Afterwards, I make sure to ice my knees (problem points after years of basketball and other sports) and to stretch again when necessary. Sometimes, especially in the winter, I'll soak in a hot bath with Epsom salt. Whether it's a legitimate homeopathic remedy for my aches or simply slick self-deception, I wind up feeling refreshed and far less banged up the next day. As long as you're doing something healthy and it works for you then keep doing it!

WORKOUT SUGGESTIONS

While I would hardly consider myself to be an expert in terms of fitness and working out I *have* accrued enough experience over the past twenty years to know my way around a gym. I've read quite a bit on the subject and have picked the brains of plenty who are far wiser and better versed in the subject than I am. As a result, I feel confident in proffering some suggestions in terms of exercises that are worth engaging in to help transform your physique.

Unfortunately, there is no perfect catch-all workout that will suit everyone. The exercises and workout approaches that I can offer serve, much like everything else in this book, merely as a starting point. I highly recommend conducting your *own* research either through reading, watching videos, or interacting directly with those who are properly trained to assist you.

With that said, the absolute most important aspect of *any* workout regimen is technique. Simply put, you are risking serious bodily harm and will never achieve maximum gains by performing exercises incorrectly. As such, maintaining proper form isn't just paramount—it's the single most critical aspect of working out.

The following are other ideas worth considering as you engage in these exercises and begin to develop your own workout regimen:

I. *Free Weights Versus Machines*

With any exercise, if there is a way to perform it using a machine and using free weights, opt for the free weights. For one, you are engaging muscles that would otherwise be rendered dormant by the machine during your repetitions. Using free weights forces you to engage certain stabilizer muscles that are key to supporting your joints and major muscles while simultaneously assisting you in performing the exercise correctly. Machines inhibit your range of motion and they detract from the physical stress that comes with utilizing proper form and technique.

II. *Gaining Mass Versus Toning Muscle*

When you are deciding what types of exercises you want to do you must also consider what your aesthetic goals are. If you're looking to bulk up then you will need to choose a particular weight range and number of sets and repetitions; if you're looking either to slim down or to tone up then both the weight and the sets and repetitions will be different. The most important thing to consider though is that your technique and form should never falter regardless of the weight that you are using.

As a general rule of thumb, if you want to put on more mass then you should be using heavier weight and performing fewer reps. If you're seeking to add more definition to your muscles then lighter weight and more reps are called for. Typically, mass-building entails performing six to eight repetitions (no more than ten) of an exercise at a weight that causes you to fail at that prescribed point without sacrificing form. For example, if you can take a pair of 35 lb. dumbbells and perform bicep curls where you absolutely cannot lift the weight another time after the sixth or seventh rep then you are in the proper range for bulking up.

Muscle toning requires a different approach that involves weight that is light enough to attain higher reps but one that is still heavy enough to give you resistance. Usually toning falls in the ten to twelve rep range with fifteen reps usually being the upper limit; if you're able to do any more than that then you are probably not using heavy enough weight. When in doubt, you can always shoot for the middle ground and aim for a weight that lets you complete ten reps but no more.

III. *Muscle Grouping*

There are myriad ways of ordering workouts but generally folks stick to one of only a handful. There are some people who work out every muscle group during each session (I still loosely count myself among them). The problem with this is that you wind up tiring out your body, increase recovery time, and decrease your overall efficiency as you reach the latter portions of your workout. I take advantage of this approach more for its time saving purposes than anything else; at this point in my life I would much rather lift at the gym twice a week for two hours at a clip than have to make four trips for an hour each time.

With that said, most people divide their workouts into complementary muscle groups. One common collection is to exercise chest (pectorals) and triceps one day, back (deltoids and lats) and biceps another day, and then shoulders (including traps) and legs another day with abdominal workouts either interspersed or designated to their own day. Another popular grouping is to do chest and arms (pectorals, biceps, and triceps together) one day, shoulders another, and then back and legs. A third is to combine chest and shoulders leaving arms and back for another day and legs unto themselves.

The reason for these groupings is the tendency for muscle groups to overlap; even though a particular muscle is the primary target of a given exercise, other complementary muscles are triggered to help complete the rep. The triceps help the pectorals and shoulders during pushing exercises while the biceps aid the back in pulling exercises. As such, working similar muscle groups on the same day will help to maximize the efficiency of your workout and allow for ample recovery time between workouts.

Please remember that any exercise regimen warrants undue consideration particularly for those who are either new to weightlifting or who have experienced a substantial delay between workouts. Please take it slow and start with a reasonable amount of weight until you are both comfortable with performing the exercises properly and have a better awareness of your physical limitations and capabilities.

For sake of ease I will group the exercises according to the primary muscle targeted. This list is far from exhaustive and is emblematic more of my own personal preferences for exercises. For anyone who is interested in exploring weightlifting to a more serious degree I would recommend checking out Arnold Schwarzenegger's and Bill Dobbins' The New Encyclopedia of Modern Bodybuilding: The Bible of Bodybuilding, Fully Updated and Revised as it goes into far greater depth on the subject than I could possibly hope to do here.

SAMPLE EXERCISES

I. *CHEST* (Pectorals)

Flat Barbell Bench Press: Lying flat on a bench that is parallel to the floor and with your feet planted firmly on the ground, grip the bar overhand with hands slightly more than shoulder-width apart. Lift and lower the bar until your elbows are at ninety degrees (don't allow the bar to make contact with your chest—if you do then you are going too low). When the bar has reached this height, squeeze your core muscles, keep your back and neck against the bench, and push the bar up as high as you can without locking out your elbows. This completes one rep.

Flat Dumbbell Bench Press: The mechanics are the same as the barbell except that you have more range of motion with the dumbbells. Make sure to engage your core and to squeeze your pectorals as you press to ensure that you are lifting the weights in a single, fluid motion and that the requisite muscles are supported properly.

Push-Up: Make your body into a straight line parallel to the floor with your hands slightly wider than shoulder width apart and your toes touching the ground. Engage your core to maintain the straight line as you lower yourself towards the ground, allowing your elbows to bow outward. Stop when your chin is only an inch or two off of the ground and then push upwards while focusing on keeping your form. When you have returned to your starting position you have completed one rep.

Dumbbell Flyes: Lying flat on a bench that is parallel to the floor and with your feet planted firmly on the ground, grip a pair of dumbbells and raise them to the highest press position. Turn your palms towards each other, bend your elbows slightly, and lower the weights in a wide arc at both sides (envision yourself opening a large newspaper to get a better idea of the movement). Return your arms to the starting position to complete one rep.

II. *TRICEPS*

Dips: Gripping a pair of dip handles or parallel bars, lift yourself up so that you are supporting your body weight with your feet off of the ground. Slowly lower yourself without allowing your neck to scrunch up (like a turtle hiding in its shell) as far as you can before pushing yourself back up into the starting position. This completes one rep.

Close Grip Bench Press: The same mechanics as a standard bench press except you grip the bar with your hands only a few inches apart (many bars have a smooth central area abutted by two rough areas. For close grip, your hands should be gripping only the smooth section with your pinkies just touching the line of demarcation between rough and smooth).

Skullcrushers: Lying on a flat bench, grip an EZ Curl Bar and raise it so that your arms are perpendicular to the floor (this would be the apex of the typical bench press movement). Keeping your elbows firmly in place and your upper arms immobile, allow your elbows to flex to lower the bar towards your face stopping when it is directly above your forehead. Be sure not to allow your elbows to flare out as you lower the weight. Again, maintaining stationary upper arms, reverse the motion to return to the starting position. This completes one rep.

Rope Pulldowns: Using a rope handle attached to a pulley machine, grip the rope tightly in both hands and stand with your feet together. Maintaining straight posture, pull down on both rope handles simultaneously, flaring them out as your arms straighten completely. Reverse the motion allowing the rope to rise until your forearms are parallel to the floor. This completes one rep.

Kick-Backs: Take a dumbbell and hold it in one hand while you place the opposite knee onto a flat bench. Lower your torso so that your back is parallel with the ground while keeping your head up looking forward. Begin with your elbow pinched tightly against your side and your forearm perpendicular to your body. Moving only your elbow, press the dumbbell backwards until your arm is straight and then lower it back to the starting position. This completes one rep.

III. BICEPS

Barbell / Dumbbell Curl: Stand with your feet shoulder-width apart, knees slightly bent, chest out, shoulders back, and a strong arch in your back to engage your core. Grip either a pair of dumbbells or a barbell with your palms facing outward. Moving only your forearms, hinge at the elbow to raise the weight in a smooth arc upward, squeezing the biceps at the top of the movement. Then, slowly lower the weight to the starting position. This completes one rep.

Incline / Decline Curls: Lying on either an incline or decline bench, grip a pair of dumbbells with palms facing upward allowing your arms to dangle at your side. Engage the biceps and hinge at the elbow moving only your forearms as you curl the dumbbells to the top of the motion before returning them to the starting position. Be sure not to allow your elbows to flare out as you move.

Standing Cable Curls: Gripping either a single handle or two individual handles attached to a pulley machine, perform a curl motion as described in the barbell / dumbbell section.

Concentration Curls: Sit down on a flat bench with a dumbbell between your feet. Bending over at the hip, place the back of your upper arm on top of your thigh and reach down with the same hand to grip the dumbbell. Keep the upper arm immobile as you contract the biceps and move only your forearm up in an arc, curling the dumbbell. Slowly lower the weight back down to complete one rep.

IV. SHOULDERS

Dumbbell Front Raise: Stand with your feet shoulder-width apart, knees slightly bent, chest out, shoulders back, and a strong arch in your back to engage your core. Hold a pair of dumbbells with an overhand grip (palms facing the floor), and, keeping it perfectly straight, slowly raise one arm in front of you until it is parallel with the floor; *DO NOT RAISE THE WEIGHT ANY HIGHER!* Once your arm is straight out in front of you, slowly lower it as you raise the other weight. When the second dumbbell returns to the starting position you have completed one rep.

Dumbbell Side Raise: Stand with your feet shoulder-width apart, knees slightly bent, chest out, shoulders back, and a strong arch in your back to engage your core. Hold a pair of dumbbells with an overhand grip (palms facing the floor), and, keeping it perfectly straight, slowly raise both arms out to your side until they are parallel with the floor; *DO NOT RAISE THE WEIGHT ANY HIGHER!* Once your arms form a straight line across your shoulders, slowly lower the weights. When the dumbbells return to the starting position you have completed one rep.

Shoulder Press: Sit upright on a bench with back support with a dumbbell in each hand. Raise the dumbbells so that they are at shoulder height with your palms facing outward. Exhaling, press the weights upward until your arms are almost fully straightened; *DO*

NOT LOCK OUT YOUR ELBOWS! Slowly inhale and lower the weights until they are again resting just at shoulder level. This completes one repetition.

Arnold Press: Sit upright on a bench with back support with a dumbbell in each hand. Raise the dumbbells so that your palms are facing you and the weights are roughly at shoulder height. Twisting your wrist, press one dumbbell upward until your arm is nearly fully straightened and your palm is now facing outward; *DO NOT LOCK OUT YOUR ELBOWS!* Slowly inhale and lower the weight, twisting your wrist so that your palm faces inward once again as you raise the second dumbbell. When the second weight returns to the starting position you have completed one rep.

V. BACK (LATS & DELTOIDS)

Pull Ups / Chin Ups: For chin ups, grip an overhead bar with palms facing inward and arms shoulder width apart; for pull ups, grip an overhead bar with palms facing outward and arms wider than shoulder width apart. Gripping the handle tightly, engage your biceps and back muscles to lift yourself higher so that your chin passes above the bar then slowly lower yourself back down to the starting position. This completes one rep.

Lat Pull Down: Grip a long handle attached to a lat pull down pulley with a wide grip and palms facing outward and pull down on the weight so that your arms are fully extended above you while you remain seated. Lean back at about a 30 degree angle and maintain the position as you pull the handle down towards your chest; only your arms should be moving. When the bar has touched your chest, slowly reverse the motion and allow your arms to straighten out. This completes one rep.

Reverse Flyes: Using a pec deck or reverse fly machine, sit with your chest against the pad and grip the handles with your palms facing down. Push the handles away from each other as you move your arms in an outward arc until they form a straight line (like with the side dumbbell raise), then return to the starting position. This completes one rep.

Bent Over Row: Take a dumbbell and hold it in one hand while you place the opposite knee onto a flat bench. Lower your torso so that your back is parallel with the ground while keeping your head up looking forward. Begin with your arm straight and the dumbbell just above the floor. Lift it straight up as you bend your elbow until your upper arm is parallel to the floor then lower the weight back down. This completes one rep.

VI. TRAPS (TRAPEZIUS)

Dumbbell Shoulder Shrugs: Gripping a pair of heavy dumbbells with palms facing each other, keep your feet shoulder width apart, knees slightly bent, chest engaged, shoulders back, and a supportive arch in your back to engage your core. Keeping your arms straight but elbows not fully locked out, shrug your shoulders so that they raise straight up as you bring your trapezius muscles towards your ears. Squeeze the traps tightly at the top of the motion, holding the position for at least a second or two before lowering back down to the starting position. This completes one rep.

VII. LEGS (QUADRICEPS, CALVES, AND HAMSTRINGS)

Squats (Quads): Grip a barbell that is supported upon your trapezius muscles. Keep your chest engaged, shoulders back, head facing forward, and back arched. Lower your rear end towards the floor without allowing your hips to move instead letting your knees travel forward while keeping them directly above your feet; *DO NOT ALLOW YOUR KNEES TO EXTEND FORWARD PAST YOUR FEET!* Keep your torso upright and your head facing forward as you continue to lower until your upper legs make contact with your lower legs, then drive the weight upward reversing the motion. This completes one rep.

Calf Raises (Calves): Stand on a block, elevated footpads, or a 45 lb. plate with your feet together and only the front half of your feet in contact with the support. Slowly lower your heels until they are below your toes and then contract your calf muscles to drive yourself upward until you are on the tips of your toes. Return to the starting position to complete one rep.

Deadlift (Hamstrings): Stand above a barbell with your feet hip-width apart and centered beneath the bar. Keep your chest engaged, shoulders back, head facing forward, and back arched as you bend at the hip to grip the bar with hands shoulder-width apart. Lower your hips and flex the knees as with a squat until your shins are touching the bar then, looking forward with chest up and back arched, stand up driving through your heels with the barbell moving upward. Continue to rise until you are almost fully erect but *DO NOT LOCK OUT YOUR KNEES!* Slowly reverse the motion while maintaining proper form until the weight touches the floor. You have completed one rep.

VIII. ABDOMINALS

Sit-Ups: Lying on your back on a mat, place your feet flat on the ground with your knees together and legs bent. Place fingertips around your ears, keep your shoulder-blades back so that your elbows are out at your sides, and contract your abdominal muscles as you fold forward keeping your feet planted firmly and your upper-body straight. Do not allow your neck or shoulders to tense up or to drive you forward; use only your abdominal muscles. Allow your chest to touch your thighs and then slowly lower yourself back to the starting position. This completes one repetition.

Crunches: Lying on your back on a mat, place your feet flat on the ground with your knees together and legs bent. Cross your arms over your chest and contract your abdominal muscles, lifting your shoulders but not your entire back off of the floor. Pause at the top of the motion while keeping your head and neck steady (looking

227

up at the ceiling throughout the exercise can help to maintain the proper position) and then slowly lower yourself back to the starting position. This completes one repetition.

Leg Lifts: Lying on your back on a mat, keep your feet together and your legs fully extended. Contract your lower abdominal muscles and keep everything but your legs stationary as you lift your legs up keeping them perfectly straight. Stop when your body forms a 90 degree angle with the soles of your feet parallel to the floor. Then, lower your feet back towards the ground but do not allow your heels to touch the floor; keep them an inch or so above the ground before raising them again. This completes one repetition.

Forearm Plank: Place your forearms on a mat with your elbows directly below your shoulders and your arms shoulder-width apart. Extend your legs behind you so that only your toes and your forearms are touching the ground. Squeeze your core muscles and glutes to help your body to form and to maintain a straight line making sure to keep your head and neck in line with your back. Hold the position for the requisite amount of time to complete one repetition.

SAMPLE ROUTINE

To create your own sample routine consider the muscle groupings suggested above and select three exercises per muscle group (where applicable). Perform three sets of ten repetitions with a weight that causes you to fail at or around the tenth rep for each exercise (sooner for muscle-building and later for muscle-toning). Here is a simple example:

(NOTE: The recommended repetition number represents the point at which you cannot perform another full movement of the exercise and is to be completed for each set.)

DAY 01 CHEST & TRICEPS

Flat Barbell Bench Press	3 sets	12 reps
Incline Barbell Bench Press	3 sets	12 reps
Push-Ups	3 sets	Max out
Skullcrushers	3 sets	12 reps
Rope Pulldowns	3 sets	12 reps
Kick-Backs	3 sets	12 reps

DAY 02 ABDOMINALS

Crunches	3 sets	12 reps
Leg Lifts	3 sets	12 reps

Forearm Plank	3 sets	Max out

DAY 03 BACK & BICEPS

Bent Over Row	3 sets	12 reps
Lat Pull Down	3 sets	12 reps
Pull Ups / Chin Ups	3 sets	Max out
Dumbbell Curl	3 sets	12 reps
Standing Cable Curls	3 sets	12 reps
Concentration Curls	3 sets	12 reps

DAY 04 LEGS

Squats	3 sets	12 reps
Calf Raises	3 sets	12 reps
Deadlift	3 sets	12 reps

DAY 05 SHOULDERS & TRAPS

Dumbbell Front Raise	3 sets	12 reps
Dumbbell Side Raise	3 sets	12 reps
Shoulder Press	3 sets	12 reps
Dumbbell Shoulder Shrugs	3 sets	12 reps

PARTING WORDS

(*THREE CHEERS FOR CRAFT BEER!*)

Craft beer served multiple purposes for me as I set about changing my life. At the most basic level it was the one treat that I refused to give up. Instead of seeking out pleasure from a variety of unhealthy sources I found something that made me happy and that I could enjoy in moderation without feeling like I was being deprived or missing out. I began to replace the empty sense of satisfaction that I had previously derived from sweets and other treats with the fulfillment of feeling better physically, emotionally, and mentally as a result of my hard work; the innate, overpowering need to consume had been replaced with the occasional desire to indulge.

Craft beer as a whole has also provided me with entertainment and a constructive direction to place my energy. I enjoy maintaining my blog The Beer Whisperers and in so doing I gain not only a creative outlet but deeper gratification as well through writing. I also enjoy traveling and photography so taking short road trips to scope out new breweries and then exploring the areas for photographic opportunities leads to further fulfillment and better mental and emotional health.

When most people think of fitness they think of it in a purely physical or athletic sense however there are many aspects of overall fitness each of which requires its own care and attention. Being physically fit is certainly a component of being healthy and happy but being mentally and emotionally fit are equally if not more important; it is very difficult to have one without the others.

It is impossible to be healthy and thus motivated to make changes in our lives without things to make us happy. The final, parting key to enacting these changes—whether it's losing weight or something less tangible—is to **have constructive passions that provide not just entertainment and enjoyment on a superficial level but deep, genuine *fulfillment***. We all need our safe-havens— the hobbies and pursuits where we can lose ourselves *while still doing something of value*. For some people it could be literal construction either artistically or through carpentry; for others it might be sports or reading.

Regardless of the specifics, this aspect of our lives should improve our emotional and mental states without detracting from our self-esteems or egos. You'll need a place to retreat to every now and again to recharge your batteries as you undertake your personal challenges so having something positive will only help you in your journey. Chowing down on fatty snacks while playing video games for hours on end might seem relaxing but it's hardly helping you to *improve* yourself and in the end will serve only to worsen your overall mental and emotional states; avoid escapism and seek fulfillment instead. Throughout *my* tough times, craft beer was the fuel that kept me going—the carrot dangling in front of my face on cold winter jogs and through sweat-soaked summer runs.

Since that auspicious moment of honesty a few Octobers ago, I haven't looked back on the old lifestyle that I finally left behind. Ultimately, that honest conversation with myself led me to join the ranks of those who made positive changes in their lives and helped me to leave behind the petulant self-pity of the past. Utilizing the keys outlined in this book I finally solved the problem of *myself.*

There is no miracle cure for losing weight *and* keeping it off nor is there anyone else who can do it for you; it comes down to *your* hard work and dedication. All of the effort in the world won't amount to much though if you're not setting yourself up to succeed. As you move forward with your weight-loss efforts, remember the ten keys that will help you to maximize your chances of achieving your goals: be honest with yourself, replace and with or, focus on moderation not deprivation, understand what you're eating and why, be cognizant of the calories in what you eat and drink and their sources, create a calorie deficit, establish a supportive environment around you, find the *right* type of exercise, have attainable goals that will motivate you along the way, and find fulfillment in a favorite pursuit.

As a final note, honesty and problem-solving are great practices for keeping us motivated but sometimes we can benefit just as much from a degree of self-forgiveness. We need to strike a balance between being hard enough on ourselves that we won't accept our previous array of pitiful excuses but not too hard that we prevent ourselves from succeeding. None of us are infallible and as such we will all make mistakes. It might be a late night fridge raid or a half-hearted run—regardless of the impetus of self-recrimination we need to allow ourselves some latitude when it comes to our errors.

What's important is not that we have failed ourselves in the past but rather that we do not *continue* to fail ourselves in the future. A single slip up is fine in isolation; if it becomes habitual then there is a problem. The key then is to identify which situation we are facing and to act accordingly. Find a way to atone for an error rather than admonish yourself to the point of lowered self-esteem; if we are being truly honest with ourselves then forgiveness will come naturally providing us with the inner harmony that is the hallmark of happy, healthy people.

FURTHER READING

AND SUGGESTED FITNESS RESOURCES

The Oxford Companion to Beer by Garrett Oliver is an outstanding compendium of all-things-beer. If you're interested in exploring the minutiae of craft beer or simply want to learn more about beer in general then this is the book for you.

How to Brew: Everything You Need To Know To Brew Beer Right The First Time by John Palmer is the de facto, definitive guide to home brewing. John manages to be extremely concise and detailed all at once with an incredibly user-friendly approach and writing style.

Extreme Brewing: An Enthusiast's Guide to Brewing Craft Beer at Home by Sam Calagione is my second favorite book about home brewing. There are a ton of useful pictures as well as several top notch recipes that you can use to replicate some of Sam's Dogfish Head branded beers or to tweak and create your own masterpiece.

Fast Food Nation by Eric Schlosser impacted me a great deal when I read it in college single-handedly ending my love affair with fast food burgers. I'd recommend checking it out if you're curious about what goes into the making of fast food. Even if you're not though I would recommend that you take the chance to go onto your favorite restaurant's website and scope out the ingredients in your preferred items as well as (and more importantly) the nutritional information. One look at the fat and sodium contents in some of these foods should be enough to have you considering better alternatives!

The New Encyclopedia of Modern Bodybuilding: The Bible of Bodybuilding, Fully Updated and Revised by Arnold Schwarzenegger and Bill Dobbins is to weight-lifting what How to Brew is to home brewing. It's the most comprehensive compendium of exercises and bodybuilding suggestions that I've ever encountered and is certainly worth the read if you're looking to take your working out more seriously.

Each of the following is something that I have personally used as a part of my weight loss journey. I am in no way affiliated with or endorsed by any of the companies or products therein nor are they aware of my appreciation of their products. They are all things that have worked for me and as such I would like to pass that information along in the hope that they will either do the same for you or will at least serve as a starting point.

The Couch to 5K Running Plan and the *C25K Mobile App* (by Zen Labs Fitness) were absolutely critical to my success in losing weight and in falling in love with running. The interface is excellent and allowed me to listen to my music while still hearing the prompts for when to walk and when to run. It is wholly worth the time and effort because its gradual pace and steady stream of support will help to propel you literally from sitting upon the couch to running a full 3.1 miles in mere weeks.

The Couch to 10K Running Trainer app by Zen Labs Fitness is the perfect point of continuation from the C25K program. The app actually begins with the 5K program, which you can skip if you've already completed it or you can combine both programs into one and do them both within the 10K Trainer app.

21K Runner app by ClearSkyApps is the program that I used to complete my first half-marathon run. I like this one better than the one offered by Zen Labs but I encourage you to shop around and see which one might best suit your needs. The Zen Labs one had a lot of

238

walking involved and by the time I got to this point I was running for at least 60 minutes every time out; the last thing that I wanted to do was to take a step backwards by having to stop arbitrarily to walk every half hour. The ClearSkyApps 21K Runner had what I felt was a better approach and so I used that to achieve my loftiest running goal to date.

BeachBody Programs like P90X, T25, and Insanity are all great, *great* ways of getting fitter and losing weight but I would hold off on scoping them out until you've gotten into a solid routine of working out. I loved P90X because of host Tony Horton's engaging patter, his encouraging support (which never got old), and the challenge of the exercises. Insanity is obviously far more challenging and I would save that for really sculpting your body down the road but it's still worth looking into. T25 keeps the workouts limited to 25 minutes while achieving an intensity level somewhere between P90X's and Insanity's. Great for those with less free time or more difficulty in fitting exercise into their daily routines!

Planet Fitness is one of my all-time favorite gyms because of the friendly, helpful environment it provides its members. Each location is designed with the beginner in mind with many new-user-friendly machines and plenty of helpful staff and trainers on hand to assist people along their weight loss journeys. The intimidation factor that many other fitness clubs have simply doesn't exist at Planet Fitness. Plus their Cybex brand of cardio machines is excellent, particularly the ArcTrainer.

Cheers and thank you for reading Beer & Fitness: The Practical Guide to Exploring Craft Beer and Improving Physical and Mental Fitness. *Sláinte!*

---

[1] http://www.cdc.gov/obesity/data/adult.html

[2] https://www.brewersassociation.org/statistics/national-beer-sales-production-data/

[3] https://www.brewersassociation.org/statistics/economic-impact-data/

[4] https://www.brewersassociation.org/statistics/number-of-breweries/

[5] https://www.sba.gov/sites/default/files/advocacy/SB-FAQ-2016_WEB.pdf

[6] https://www.brewersassociation.org/statistics/number-of-breweries/

[7] http://www.inc.com/inc5000/list/2015/

[8] http://www.agiweb.org/geotimes/aug04/resources.html

[9] https://en.wikipedia.org/wiki/Malting_process

[10] https://en.wikipedia.org/wiki/Beer

[11] https://en.wikipedia.org/wiki/Yeast#Beer

[12] https://en.wikipedia.org/wiki/Brewing#Fermentation_methods

[13] https://en.wikipedia.org/wiki/Ale

[14] https://en.wikipedia.org/wiki/Saccharomyces_cerevisiae

[15] https://olis.leg.state.or.us/liz/2013R1/Measures/Overview/HCR12

[16] https://en.wikipedia.org/wiki/Brettanomyces

[17] http://www.howtobrew.com/section3/chapter17.html

[18] https://en.wikipedia.org/wiki/Lautering

[19] Michael Lewis, Tom W. Young (2002). *Brewing*. Springer. p. 272

[20] Charles W. Bamforth (9 September 2011). *The Oxford Companion to Beer*. pp. 141–142. ISBN 9780195367133.

[21] Michael J. Lewis, Charles W. Bamforth (4 October 2006). *Essays in Brewing Science*. Springer. p. 47. ISBN 9780387330105.

[22] http://morebeer.com/brewingtechniques/library/backissues/issue2.1/tinseth.html

[23] https://en.wikipedia.org/wiki/Hops

[24] http://www.howtobrew.com/section1/chapter5-1.html

[25] "Handbook of brewing - Google Books". books.google.co.uk.

[26] https://en.wikipedia.org/wiki/Brewing#Wort_cooling

[27] https://en.wikipedia.org/wiki/Brewing#Wort_cooling

[28] http://www.howtobrew.com/section1/chapter6-9-3.html

[29] *Brewing* By Michael Lewis, Tom W. Young. ISBN 0306472740 p. 298

[30] http://www.wikihow.com/Brew-Commercial-Beer

[31] Keith Thomas (7 October 2011). *The Oxford Companion to Beer*. Oxford University Press. ISBN 9780195367133.

[32] http://www.howtobrew.com/section1/chapter8-3.html

[33] http://www.craftbrewingbusiness.com/equipment-systems/bright-beer-tanks-reviewed-by-stone-brewings-mitch-steele/

[34] http://blog.beeriety.com/2009/08/03/what-is-bottle-conditioned-beer/

[35] http://www.morebeer.com/content/using_oak_in_beer

[36] https://www.brewersassociation.org/statistics/craft-brewer-defined/

[37] https://www.brewersassociation.org/statistics/market-segments/

[38] http://www.craftbeer.com/craft-beer-muses/nano-breweriesmdash-talk-of-the-craft-beer-nation

[39] http://insidescoopsf.sfgate.com/blog/2014/04/18/lagunitas-brewing-company-had-a-really-big-year/

[40] https://www.brewersassociation.org/statistics/national-beer-sales-production-data/

[41] http://www.mensjournal.com/food-drink/drinks/the-man-who-dumps-more-beer-than-most-brewers-produce-20141121

[42] http://www.morebeer.com/articles/brewing_with_adjuncts

[43] https://en.wikipedia.org/wiki/K%C3%B6lsch_%28beer%29

[44] http://www.beeradvocate.com/beer/style/101/

[45] https://en.wikipedia.org/wiki/Trappist_beer

[46] https://en.wikipedia.org/wiki/Dubbel

[47] http://www.pastemagazine.com/articles/2014/10/the-expanding-demographics-of-craft-beer.html

[48] https://www.cdc.gov/healthyschools/obesity/facts.htm

[49]

http://www.heart.org/HEARTORG/HealthyLiving/HealthyKids/ChildhoodObesity/Overweight-in-Children_UCM_304054_Article.jsp

[50] https://www.cdc.gov/nchs/fastats/obesity-overweight.htm

[51] http://www.entenmanns.com/op-prod.cfm/prodid/7203000809#.VnCH_r82fMo

[52] http://www.pepperidgefarm.com/PopNutrition.aspx?prdID=120278&catID=773

[53] http://www.myfitnesspal.com/tools/bmr-calculator

Made in the USA
Middletown, DE
26 April 2017